# The Psychology of Fear of Love

**The Divided Self Series, Volume 2**

christine joanna hart

Published by Pale Horse Press, 2026.

THE PSYCHOLOGY OF FEAR OF LOVE

**First edition. March 30, 2026.**



ISBN: 979-8233025297

Written by christine joanna hart.

# Table of Contents

"To RJ for what will always remain."

*"For one human being to love another; that is perhaps the most difficult of all of our tasks." -*

**Rainer Maria Rilke.**

**Christine Joanna Hart** is a certified investigative psychotherapist and writer with a background in frontline journalism, criminal profiling, and psychotherapeutic training. Her bylines include investigations in The Sunday Times and Daily Mail. Publishing her personal memoir of childhood abuse propelled Hart to Sunday Times bestseller status with Hodder & Stoughton. She has been featured as a guest on BBC World Service, BBC TV, GMTV, and BBC Radio, speaking on topics including childhood trauma and serial murder.

# Praise for C J Hart's writing.

**Val Hennessy, Daily Mail.** 'If only Hart had a better editor; we might have the best book ever written about a childhood.

**Doug White, reviewer, News of The World** – 'Reminiscent of Silence of the Lambs – hard to put down.' *****

**Jim Dole; editor, Sunday World.** 'This is Lady

Chatterley's Lover, in the shadow of a gunman instead of a Game-Keeper.

**Prohibition Magazine**

'An uplifting true story about courage and loneliness, a real page-turner.' * * * * *

**Lancashire Times.** A salute to the struggle made by the author throughout her life. This is a perfect guide for anyone suffering from adoption or family problems.' * * * *

**Henry Mc Donald – Observer** - Good story throughout, but more Mills and 'BOOM!' than Mills and Boon.

**Christopher Berry-Dee, author of Talking with Serial Killers.**

A super and rather unusual book. Well written with plenty of personal anecdotes. What appeals to me, as it will anyone with an interest in true crime, is Hart's unique talent in 'accessing all areas', specifically getting to interview Kenneth Alessio Bianchi, aka, 'The Hillside Strangler'. She will have her critics, of course, and we all do, but Hart not only talks-the-talk, she walks the-walk, and spent years corresponding with Bianchi before, at great expense, she visited with him at the Washington State Penitentiary, Walla Walla. Having dealt with Bianchi, on a one-one-one basis myself, this serial killer, and master-manipulator is not someone to trifle with.

**CHRISTINE JOANNA HART**

As the author of a score of books on serial homicide and a media consultant on the subject - two of my books are required reading by students at the FBI's Behavioural Science Unit, Quantico, VA.

I would say that Hart's research on serial killers is a must-read, most especially for any student with an interest in the psychology of serial murder. *****

# THE PSYCHOLOGY OF FEAR OF LOVE

Published in the United Kingdom by Pale Horse Press.



A catalogue record for this book is available from the British Library.

# Chapter One: The Widower.

*"The rose speaks of love silently, in a language only the heart understands."*
*— Unknown*

*

South Belfast. A city rinsed with rain and the memory of fire.

Chrissy Hart, 34, psychotherapist, lit her last Marlboro Gold of the night and leaned against the cold granite counter of her kitchen, a single pendant bulb above casting a soft, milky circle of light.

She held the cigarette in a long black holder, the kind she'd bought from an antique stall on the Lisburn Road to try to bring some atmosphere into her mundane existence. It reminded her of smoky Parisian brothels she'd never visited but imagined vividly.

The kitchen smelt faintly of white paint, lemon disinfectant, and something metallic from the old pipes. She wore a soft green cardigan, frayed at the sleeve, faux ballet slipper pumps with thinning soles, and nothing else beneath the cardigan but a silk camisole the colour of old cream.

She'd meant to write some more of her unfinished novel today, truly. But the rain.

Rainfall rattled against the wide sash windows like impatient fingers, persistent, cold. It left trails down the panes like tears, and outside the garden blurred into a pool of greys. The old ash tree in the garden was skeletal. It had held onto its leaves like stubborn lovers but now stood bare, accusing the sky.

A shiver rippled through her and she hugged her favourite green cardigan tighter, glancing up at the gorgeous chandelier she'd hung herself last week: orange iron petals, a stem of tarnished gold, and a cascade of filigree. It looked too lavish for the living room, which still smelt faintly of Farrow and Ball, Indian Yellow paint, but she adored it.

The house; her rented manor in South Belfast; was far too big for just her. A Victorian relic with ceilings like church vaults, ancient radiators that hissed like gossiping women, and oak floorboards that creaked as though someone were always pacing somewhere just out of view. It was far cheaper than London prices she was so used to; so, she'd signed up for a year with a clause to buy it at the end of the year if she still liked it.

At night, when the wind howled through the eaves, it whistled as if the house were speaking in a long-dead tongue. She sometimes imagined ghosts behind the dark wardrobe doors when insomnia hit.

She'd tried to warm the house with brown leather settees, Turkish rugs, an old bookcase filled with true crime and classic novels she loved; The Secret History, The Bell Jar, The Road to Wigan Pier. Still, the place felt like it watched her more than she watched it. A great beast of a house, lonely as she was.

She sipped her Rioja: deep, dark, and plummy, with the faintest curl of smoke on the tongue. It stained her lips as she wandered from kitchen to hallway.

She could hear the annoying little dog barking next door again; scrappy little thing with a yap that chipped away at her nerves. She sighed. No man. No child. Just the whine of a neighbour's mutt and a half-written book about forbidden love.

She'd met a terrorist commander once; in her career as an investigative journalist; in a safe house. Sharp cheekbones, hard blue grey eyes, scars on his knuckles. He'd been polite, enigmatic, and utterly unreachable. She was fresh from London and a ten-year stetch with the Daily Mail as a true crime investigative reporter.

When she reached her thirties, it had seemed too much to continue as a newspaper reporter: the ever-present threat of violence. She wanted to investigate people's minds! So, she studied hard, a degree in Psychology and then a Diploma to open her own Psychotherapeutic Practice.

Her home was in St Ives, Cornwall, yet, Ireland felt like a cosy warm place to begin a practice, it was familiar and friendly and she recalled it from her years as a hack. There was also a mad idea to write a great love story. Chrissy harboured the belief that all grand love stories were of forbidden love; Wuthering Heights, Sons and Lovers; and so, the idea came to her that she would pen a novel about the forbidden love between an English journalist and an Irish man of terror.

It was a ridiculous idea of course because the English wouldn't ever identify with it, but for some reason it stuck in her head as a fantastic commercial enterprise that would lift her out of the endless drudgery of non-stop writing and into a Jackie Collins lifestyle of St Tropez beaches and million-pound yachts parked just off shore.

Her grand plan hit a sticky wicket; men of terror didn't have love affairs with journalists. Not unless you wanted to wake up dead.

But it was that very distance that fascinated her: the lines between ethics and desire, story and reality. She was desperate to write a story that mattered, but it had to be real. She called it *method* writing.

And so, she'd gone out that rainy lonely Saturday night to the Lisburn Road Club with Pauline and Nadine; her head full of discontent and hopeless dreams of becoming a mix of Agatha Christie and D H Lawrence.

Soon as she entered the centrally placed nightclub called Madison's she felt her spirits lift. The bar staff made the best Black Russians in Belfast! She grinned over at her friends as they stood by the dance floor quaffing Pepsi and Kahlua cocktails. Both of whom worked in nursing, wore glittery dresses and chewed gum like they were still in secondary school.

The parochial Belfast night club was smoky, stale with spilt lager and too much Avon perfume. Nothing like the sophistication of London clubs. There were cheesy hits from the early 2000s, a sticky, beer slicked dance floor, and clusters of older men in short-sleeved shirts. She almost laughed. Until she saw him.

He was leaning at the end of the bar, navy designer suit crumpled, a crystal-coloured silk tie loosened at his throat. His hair was dark and silky, slicked back like he'd stepped from a 1950s photograph. He looked like a dream; a man out of a movie; out of a novel written years ago but still sacred. She felt her breath quicken and her fingers tightened around the cocktail glass.

His skin was pale, jaw clean and sharp. He wasn't beautiful: he was arresting. Something devilish flickered around his mouth, and his eyes were the bluest she'd ever seen with a ring of antique yellow gold at the very centre. Not soft blue. Storm blue. Eyes that knew something you didn't.

She stared at him for far too long and he turned, holding her gaze. She walked straight over.

"Where are you from?" she asked hoping she'd sound friendly rather than interrogational.

He smiled slowly, eyes raking her green cardigan.

"Tyrone."

Perfect. Her mind whirred. She could see her book opening right there. First chapter; the wilds of Ireland.

"I'm writing a book," she said boldly.

He lifted one brow. "I could drive you about Tyrone. Show you the wildest glens if you like."

She laughed. "Are you offering to be my free tour guide?"

"Aye, maybe. What kind of book is it?"

"A book about forbidden love-making called, Unreal in Love."

She studied his face, lit golden by the bar's low lighting. He smelt of oud and musk, with something deeper beneath; dark wood, maybe amber. It caught in her throat.

There was an imediate and intense physical attraction and they had both drunk cocktails, so flirting was easy. As they danced in the dimly-lit nightclub below the busy bar into the small hours, his hand rested lightly on the small of her back. His body moved with hers like they'd done this before. At one point, he leaned in close, breath warm near her ear. She turned away before their lips touched.

"Not yet," she whispered completely drunk on the strong cocktails called 'Black Russians' yet aware that he was the best-looking man she'd seen in a long time.

"Robert," he said, pressing his number into her palm like a relic and insisting he gave her his. She felt somehow determined to never let him go now she'd found him; there seemed something horrific about that ...and she imagined herself searching for him if she didn't tie him down and tag him right there and then.

Back in her rented home, she walked barefoot along the hallway, mug of camomile tea and honey in hand. The silence in the big old wooden house pressed against her.

Upstairs, in her vast bedroom with its muted orange walls and heavy curtains the colour of dried blood, she sat at the edge of the bed, looking out through the rain misted window. Her ballet pump slippers hung off her feet.

The wind picked up outside, and somewhere in the pipes, something knocked. She wrapped her green cardigan around her like armour, then stood, lit another cigarette, and whispered to the dark:

"*Method writing!* Maybe I feel so strongly about this stranger because he'll clearly help me get this love story novel written. He'll drive me around Tyrone. He's drop dead gorgeous and might well be the muse who brings out the best-selling novelist in me!"

She grinned then suddenly glimpsed herself from a reflection in an antique brass mirror; she'd become brittle.

Maybe it was all the years working as a journalist on Fleet Street where it was dog eat dog and men treated you badly. She'd become intensely self-protective; she had barriers of steel around her heart.

It was ok to think of the dark-haired mystery man as if he was an accessory: a way of getting this novel finally written; after all she had

Robert Kirby; a top literary agent telling her she had a skill to write thrillers like no other.

But what if this dark-haired hunk was something magical; a real chance at love. Then wouldn't she be able to write an amazing book about a 'Fifty Shades of Grey,' type affair with him in the green glens of Ireland anyway!

As she stared at her reflection, she realised that the idea of experiencing true love absolutely scared the shit out of her.

She felt extremely old in her mid-thirties, she felt as if she was an old princess still hoping to get married and have the entire thing of kids, a home, normality.

It felt safe to pretend she didn't want what every other woman seemed to have gotten so easily got for themselves; it felt safer to reach for the Jackie Collins high life.

Wouldn't that make her far superior to other women?

Couldn't she look down at them and laugh when she achieved the yacht, the billion pounds villa in Los Angeles and the international best seller made into a movie starring Ben Affleck and Jennifer Lopez! She gulped some more hot tea and saw a coward staring right back at her. Other women could risk pain and rejection and she... just couldn't.

No, this Robert would be a project. He would be a means to and end. And that was why she was excited.

***

The slow wintry week came and went and he still hadn't rung. She was busy thinking about running her fingers through his dark silky hair daily and what it'd smell like on her fingers afterwards.

"What the fuck anyway!" She started to Nadine down the phone. "I had so many black Russians I bet he doesn't even look anything like I remember. I bet it was all sexual fantasy on my part."

"Well, I didn't see him, but you pointed him out to Pauline so she might recall; but then I doubt it: she was drunk out of her mind!"

"Yeah well, she got the wrong guy. I sent her over to ask where he came from. She got the wrong guy... so I had to go over and do it myself!"

"Sounds like Pauline alright!"

"O' Nadine! We don't meet men we like, do we. He had this real enigmatic persona; ivory skin, sapphire eyes and this charming connection to deep wild nature. Something feral I've never even seen before in any other man."

'God, you've got it bad; mind if I vomit?"

They both shrieked with laughter and suddenly the fact he hadn't rung didn't mean the worst because after all she had his number and she'd chase him down if she had to. He was far too special to let just fly away.

***

**Authors Clinical Observations:** When I wrote this chapter, I believed I was writing a love story based on Robert and I; a love story I found unbelievable painful.

Looking back, I can see I was circling something else entirely.

I had met a widower; a man already haunted by a ghost and I entered that story as if ghosts were safer than living women. At the time, I would not have said that. I would have said I was romantic, drawn to tragedy, intoxicated by intensity.

But intensity was not the truth.

Distance was.

A widower is the safest unavailable man of all. His heart is already occupied. There is a built-in third presence. I did not have to arrive fully in my body. I could drift, aestheticise, narrate, observe. I could be half-there and call it mystery.

I had grown up without sovereignty over my own body. My boundaries were not respected. My "no" did not function. So as an adult, embodiment felt dangerous. To be fully present in desire felt like stepping into exposure without armour.

Instead, I chose stories where longing could remain suspended.

Notice how I describe myself here; cinematic, lit by rain, cigarette holder, dramatic light. I am performing atmosphere rather than inhabiting myself. That was dissociation masquerading as personality.

I believed great love must be tragic because tragedy allowed me to feel without surrendering control. If love is doomed, I never have to risk full presence.

What I could not see then was this: I felt unreal in relationships because I had dimmed myself long before I met him.

The ghost was not his dead wife.

*The ghost was me.*

# Chapter Two – Waiting.

*Lily of the Valley: Associated with the return of happiness, these small, bell-shaped flowers carry the scent of lost mornings and forgotten laughter.*

*

The gas fire hissed as it came to life, casting a golden flicker over her brown leather settees, her favourite she'd bought from a shop in Ormeau Road: it had character. She curled her feet beneath her under a grey furry throw and stared at the half-finished chapter on her laptop screen.

*Unreal in Love.* A working title, but somehow fitting. The kind of title that made people sigh a little before they even turned the first page. Only... how could she write about love when she'd never, ever fallen into it herself?

Rain ran in silver veins down the tall sash windows. Outside, the January sky was the colour of pewter, thick and lidless, and inside the house, Chrissy pulled on her cardigan, soft from wear, sleeves a little too long, and her ballet slippers made no sound against the creaky wooden floors. The room still smelled faintly of last night's fish n' chip supper.

At night, the house changed; the wind moved through the floorboards and under the doors, whispering like an old friend who had secrets to tell. The high ceilings and cold walls made her feel like she was living in a memory; someone else's life she had moved into. A woman long dead. Some evenings she swore she heard her sigh.

She lit a candle on the table, cinnamon and clove, and poured herself a glass of red: Château de Berne, a ruby-coloured wine that warmed her chest like velvet. She had meant to write another twenty pages today. Instead, she had only managed one page and wandered the halls barefoot, listening to the annoying little dog bark next door, the radio murmuring old jazz, her thoughts drifting to him: Robert.

Her phone buzzed. Nadine.

Chrissy picked up. "Hey!"

"You writing or brooding?"

"A bit of both."

There was a pause.

"Catch yourself on," Nadine ordered. "You're not going to write a real love story until you've been properly, irretrievably in love."

Chrissy let out a dry laugh. "I know. You've to have kissed someone so hard your knees turned to jelly. You've to have done stupid things like make love naked in the rain."

"Exactly! Wuthering Heights. Anna Karenina. All the messed-up ones."

"I've never experienced that," Chrissy said, curling her knees tighter to her chest. "I've never, ever been kissed in the rain, or fought for someone like my life depended on it."

"Then maybe it's time you did."

Chrissy gazed into her glass. "Well, I think the man I met is a someone. Kind of."

"Kind of?"

"At Madison's last Saturday. He looked like..." she hesitated, "like a someone."

"Oh Jesus, the blue-eyed wonder! The one you were dancing with! He looked like trouble in a suit."

"He smelled like oud and something woody; like musk and danger."

"Did he even call?"

Chrissy frowned. "No, no, he didn't call. But I got his number."

"Married then."

"No," Chrissy said softly. "Widowed."

"Oh no. That's a terrible idea. Widowers are bad news."

"I know. They haven't fallen out of love with their wives. They were taken. He'll still be madly in love with another woman. And that woman will have owned his whole heart"

"Exactly. So why bother?"

'I don't know; I can't help my feelings."

"Well, we shouldn't listen to our feelings; we should have discipline. My feelings would allow me to drink an entire bottle of wine a night if I let them!

Chrissy nodded but the memory of his hand on her back during the slow dance lingered. The smell of his rich woody cologne, that slight hesitation before he almost kissed her, then didn't. He'd passed her his number on a torn bit of paper, handwritten. *Robert.*

***

The next morning, Chrissy met Nadine and Pauline for a late breakfast, more of a brunch at the café along Lisburn Road at the very top of Belvedere Road. The smell of frying eggs and roasted coffee drifted through the open door, and rain had already started again, slicking the pavement, dotting the windows.

Inside, it was all steamed glass and clinking cutlery. Chrissy had her usual; scrambled eggs on sourdough, butter dripping down the side, and a flat white. Nadine had pancakes. Pauline was on a detox and only drank nettle tea.

"I don't know how you function without proper food," Chrissy muttered, cutting into the buttery toast.

"You mean booze. You had five Black Russians last Saturday, didn't you?" Pauline smirked. "Classy."

"It matched my mood."

"So... are you going to call *him*? Since he hasn't called you?"

Chrissy glanced down at her iPhone. *Robert.* Saved under that one name.

"He said he'd show me around Tyrone."

"You're not seriously going to let a stranger drive you around the countryside, are you?" Nadine arched an eyebrow.

Chrissy stirred her flat white. "It's method writing."

"Method madness."

Across the café, Chrissy caught sight of a copper she knew; Chief Inspector Eric Anderson. Broad-shouldered, silver-haired, reading the Irish Times with one hand and sipping tea with the other.

"There's Eric Anderson, I might not be a hack anymore but I still appreciate a cop contact," she announced, standing up.

"No," Nadine hissed. "Sit down. Don't be mad."

"I'm a journalist by blood."

"You're never relaxed; you mad woman."

Chrissy grinned, grabbed her coat and walked toward the copper a piece of sourdough hanging out of her mouth.

On her way back home, the wind tore down the street in a cold breath, and a thought flickered through her: *Call him.* She pulled the mobile out of her woollen coat pocket and pressed on Robert.

It rang once.

"Hello?" His voice was curious and low; a little husky.

She stopped walking and felt breathless.

"Is that Robert?"

How weird to call a stranger and act as if you know them as if you have a right to be intruding on them on the basis that they might find you attractive, she thought anxiously.

Pause. "It is."

"I'm Chrissy. From the other: I mean from last Saturday night in the nightclub."

Another pause. "Aye, I remember."

"I was just ..."

"Can I buy you lunch?"

She sighed. He had let her off the hook.

"I'd love that."

***

The cold January rain had stopped by morning, but the sky had stayed a brooding grey: flat and featureless, like a blank note shoved through the letterbox.

Chrissy sat at the kitchen table in her nightdress, hunched over a plate of cold chips with brown sauce. She didn't know why she'd fried them. She hadn't even been hungry then. It was something to do. Something warm. Something that smelled like Saturday.

The house was far too quiet. Not the comfortable quiet of peace, but that buzzing sort of silence, the kind that presses on your ears until you want to scream or smash something just to hear the sound. Upstairs, the big bed was unmade. It always looked wrong, somehow. Too big. Too marital.

It had taken her a month to find those crisp Egyptian cotton sheets..."for hotel-quality sleep," the woman in the Belfast shop had said; but now they only made the loneliness look neater. At night, Chrissy lay on just one side. The other remained untouched, pristine, like a sexy glossy bed in a show home; mocking her with its luxury chocolate fur throw.

Now she couldn't even sleep without a glass of red wine, not properly. She didn't drink much at night; just a glass. Sometimes two. And it wasn't even about the alcohol. It was the ritual: the pop of the cork, the glug into the glass, the first sip. Velvet and sharp. A lullaby in a bottle.

Outside her window, the neighbours were washing their car together. A man and a woman. Matching navy anoraks. Laughing over a wet sponge. It was so domestic, so boring, and yet something in her ached for it. Not the cold damp sponge or the shiny car; but the togetherness. The casualness of love that had stayed solid.

Chrissy pulled her cardigan tighter around her. She'd bought it from a second-hand shop in Camden years ago. It smelled like lavender and old books. It still had a tiny burn mark on one sleeve from a clumsy cigarette at a protest in London. Her adoptive father had hated protests. He'd hated most things; especially her. She was adopted at age four. Her memories before that were dim, but the feeling remained. Unwanted. Forgotten. Wrong.

Men had always confused her. She'd spent years attracted to the wrong ones; men like her father: hard-eyed men with sharp smiles and pasts they couldn't talk about.

She'd interviewed paramilitaries. Sat across from them in small rooms with low light and smelt gun oil and cologne. Some were polite. Some weren't. She always kept her guard up. But part of her: some strange broken bit, was drawn to them. Men who smelled of cigarettes and pine forests and danger.

But right now, she didn't want danger. She wanted something warm. Safe. Honest. A man who made fried eggs on Sunday morning and laughed at silly jokes. A man who'd hold her hand without irony.

Later that day, she met Nadine and Pauline in town. They were sitting outside a French café in wool coats and sunglasses like two war-weary film stars from the 90s.

"You look like death warmed up," Pauline announced cheerfully.

"I feel like microwaved soup," Chrissy grinned and winked.

"Up late last night?"

"Not even. Just thinking."

They sipped frothy cappuccinos with a spray of cinnamon on top. Nadine was going on about her latest serious patient, some spiritual coach who thought he was the reincarnation of Rumi.

"And I'm like, mate, you're from Croydon, and your name's Steve. Calm down."

Chrissy laughed, but it faded quickly. The wind picked up. She tucked her red stripy scarf around her neck.

"I've advertised for clients to therapise now for over a month and I still don't have any patients."

The table went quiet. A pigeon landed near Pauline's foot.

"It'll change," Nadine said softly. "That's how I knew I had to change everything in my life. Being happy; being single was a big thing I looked at. "

Chrissy nodded, but didn't say anything.

Back home, the post had arrived. Just bills and an advert for double glazing. She threw them on the counter and opened the fridge. Empty except for a lump of cheddar and a half-drunk bottle of red. She poured a glass. Sat on the stairs. Listened to the silence again.

From her front window, she could see the houses across the street. Lights going on. Curtains drawn. A woman holding a baby. A man leaning to kiss her cheek.

She felt like she was an actress watching a film she hadn't been cast in. She whispered aloud, to no one: *I don't want to be alone forever, or poor forever, or always in rented homes.*

Then she took the glass upstairs, climbed into the too-big bed, and lay down. Tonight, she let herself sleep in the middle. She cried because life hadn't turned out how she thought that it would; a house, a continuous career, a community, parents who loved her, a partner.

She cried because it had all been a bit horrible and harsh and dark. She cried because a heart throb called Robert had invited her for lunch and it felt magical; it felt like what she knew most other women had felt when they met their husbands; a sense of magic, a feeling of inner joy ...a kind of a knowing that *this is it*; that he is *the one.*

But then the fear that he might not show up.

***

**Author's Clinical Notes:** When I wrote this chapter, I thought I was describing romantic anticipation.

I can see now I was describing dissociation.

Notice how she says she feels like an actress watching a film she hasn't been cast in.

That line is not poetic decoration.

It is diagnostic.

To feel like an actress in your own life is to experience self as performance rather than presence.

I was not inside my body.

I was observing myself from slightly above it.

That floaty quality had followed me since childhood.

When sovereignty fractures early; when your body is not safe territory — the psyche adapts by stepping half a foot outside of itself. You live near your skin, not in it. You narrate your life instead of inhabiting it.

Waiting becomes easier than arriving.

Longing becomes safer than fulfilment.

Notice how intensely she projects onto Robert before he has done anything at all. The idea of him becomes mythic. The lunch invitation becomes destiny.

That is not love.

That is fantasy filling absence.

Why widowers?

Because a widower carries a built-in third presence; a ghost who already owns part of the emotional landscape. With a widower, you never have to be fully chosen in the present. There is always a triangulation.

If someone else once owned his heart, then you are never fully responsible for inhabiting the space. You can hover.

Waiting is a strategy.

If he does not call, you remain suspended.

If he calls, you panic that he might not show up.

If he shows up, you fear you are not real enough to stay.

This is the nervous system of someone who learned early that belonging can be revoked.

## THE PSYCHOLOGY OF FEAR OF LOVE

When she whispers, "I don't want to be alone forever or poor forever, always in rented homes," she is not simply fearing loneliness.

She is fearing impermanence.

Rented homes.

Rented love.

Rented belonging.

If you never feel fully embodied, you never feel fully installed.

So, you wait.

You wait for a man to choose you.

You wait for a career to solidify.

You wait for the magical moment that makes you real.

And while you wait, you aestheticise.

You romanticise tragedy.

You idealise Wuthering Heights.

You believe love must be dramatic to count.

Intensity replaces solidity.

But here is what I could not see at 34:

I did not feel unreal because men were unavailable.

I felt unreal because I was not fully inside myself.

When the body has been locked down to survive early violation, desire becomes complicated. You want to be chosen. You want to be kissed hard enough that your knees buckle. You want mythic union.

But you also fear embodiment.

So, you choose men who carry distance.

Men who are partially elsewhere.

Men whose hearts are already occupied.

Men you can project onto.

Then you wait.

Waiting protects you from the terror of full arrival.

Because full arrival requires presence.

And presence requires sovereignty.

At the end of this chapter, she cries because she believes life has not turned out as it should have.

House.

Career.

Partner.

Community.

What she does not yet understand is that solidity does not come from being chosen by someone else.

It comes from inhabiting yourself fully.

A ghost does not accumulate.

A ghost does not root.

A ghost does not feel deserving of permanence.

And at this point in my life, I was still half-ghost.

Not because I was weak.

Because I had survived by leaving my body.

This book is not about a widower.

It is about what happens when a woman waits her whole life to be installed and finally realises she must install herself.

# Chapter Three: Robert.

*Violet: Shy and mourning, the violet has always bent its head toward grief ... and yet still smells of spring.*

It was Wednesday.

The farmhouse lay buried in the folds of the borderlands, that no-man's land of Tyrone where the hills rolled in old Gaelic hush and the earth seemed to lose its accent; falling into a silence more ancient than speech. It sat at the end of a dirt road no one used anymore, the kind of path the wind forgets to follow.

The house itself hunched low, as though it had been listening for too long. Wind-bitten trees stood above it like sentries, their bark scored by years of invisible battles. The windows were thin and watchful. Ivy crowded the lintels. The garden was a tangle of stubborn growth; nettles, docks, the last ghosts of foxglove; all of it soaked in the sour green smell of rain on rust.

An old tap dripped with the slow patience of grief. Buckets were stacked beneath it like offerings. And just beside the door, hanging from a crooked nail, was a single coat, greyed and heavy with weather, as if its owner had only stepped inside for a moment; but never returned.

Inside, it was spare; not clean, just uncared for.

The sort of emptiness that accumulates not from minimalism, but from slow disappearance. The furniture looked half-packed, as though someone had once planned to leave; maybe for a week, maybe forever and then quietly forgot how. A kettle rested on the old range, the kind that ticks softly to itself. A plastic souvenir magnet from Donegal held up a photograph of a dark-haired girl in a school uniform; smiling, mid-laugh, eyes caught on someone outside the frame.

The half grandfather clock on the mantel still worked, barely. It ticked with that tired persistence grief gives to the living.

Robert stood in the kitchen, sleeves rolled to the elbow, frying crispy cheese pancakes. They hissed in the pan like rain hitting a hot roof. The air filled with the unmistakable smell of processed cheese; too sharp, too chemical, the kind that clings to fabric long after the eating is done.

He moved like a man underwater, slow and deliberate, flipping the pancakes with careful hands, as if their golden skins might tear and spill some precious thing.

Some days, he told himself he made them for his teenage daughter Kira and son, Jon. Other days, he wasn't sure who he was feeding anymore.

"Kira!" he called. "They're ready."

No reply.

He turned down the heat and pushed his knuckles against his eyes. Sleep had been a ghost lately; hovering, whispering, never staying. He hadn't really eaten since last Tuesday.

It was Wednesday now. He thought it might be Thursday. He wasn't sure.

The girl came down the stairs. Long dark hair, eyes like his dead wife. She moved too quickly, all jangling keys and heavy boots.

"Eat something, would you?"

She grabbed a pancake with her fingers, burned herself, cursed, laughed.

"Where are you going?"

"Out."

"You were out last night."

"Jesus, dad, I'm not ten."

He stepped forward, blocking the hallway.

"Who's driving?"

"Friends."

"Which friends?"

"The ones you feckin' hate."

He glanced down at the plastic bottle in her hand; clear liquid sloshing. The label torn.

She smiled like the end of a joke and brushed past him.

Outside, a battered white VW waited at the gate. A lout of a boy in the driver's seat revved the engine too loud.

Robert didn't move. He stood there, watching the car eat her up and vanish into the misty morning.

The silence returned.

He sat down heavily at the kitchen table. The pancakes hissed quietly on the plate, cooling. He stared at them. One had split at the edge: yellow goo leaking like an ulcer.

He rubbed his face. He hadn't shaved in days. His chest ached. There was a knock at the back door. He stood slowly, opened it. A woman stood there; round face, knitted cardigan, Tupperware in her hands.

"Just dropped by. Made that beef stew you liked. Thought you might need..."

She didn't finish the sentence. She didn't have to. Robert took the container from her, muttered a thanks.

She stepped inside without waiting.

"I did some washing, too. Your sheets were damp; felt mouldy. I've seen to it."

He didn't answer.

She moved through the house like it was hers. Put things in cupboards. Straightened the tea towels. Lit a scented candle. Robert sat back down. Watched her move.

"I brought you a Tesco carrot cake."

He looked at her, then at the chicken stew, and the cake; then at the tea towels. Something shifted in his stomach.

"Jade, I don't want you doing all this."

She smiled. "Doing what?"

"This. All this."

"I'm not doing anything."

"I don't want it."

The smile dropped.

"I'm just being kind; since your wife died."

"Jade; I don't need...."

He stood up again, far too quickly, the chair scraping against the tiles. She stepped back; lips tight; picked up her bag, nodded once, and left. She reminded him of a river stoat he once spotted in a field; she was all about her own needs and getting them met; yet she'd mastered the art of appearing focussed on being helpful and giving.

When the door closed, the house exhaled.

Silence rushed back in like cold water. Robert stood still for a long time. The grandfather style clock ticked on the mantel. Loud. He'd never noticed how loud it was.

His eyes drifted to the shelf above the stove. There was a bottle there. Brown glass, dusty label. Something he'd taken from the chemist's years ago. Kept meaning to throw it out. He took it down. Held it. The label was smudged. Faded script. A word that could mean anything.

He ran his thumb over the seal. The house was too quiet. The chicken stew smelled of onions. The clock said six-thirty. Outside, the wind changed direction. He set the bottle down. Turned away. Then turned back. Looked at it again and felt loneliness swell up inside of him. He had to drive to Belfast to take out a strange woman on a date and he felt heavy and listless. What had made him do it?

A single navy Barbour coat, the fabric gone thin at the elbows, hangs from the crooked nail by the door like a mute sentinel. It leans a little toward the yellow kitchen as if it, too, is listening for footsteps that will never come and every time the door shifts in its swollen frame the coat sways, small, sorrowful.

Beneath it, the rug Serafina once beat against the hedge is worn to the grain; the weave shows where her slippers traced a thousand midnight feedings, where toddlers once toddled.

A cracked mug; her favourite, lilies fading around the lip sits beside a cold crust of burnt toast, its rim crowded with dust like a forgotten offering. Even the clock on the mantel ticks with an exhausted limp, its second hand pausing now and then as though time itself cannot quite go on without her.

The greasy scent of processed cheese blankets the stale air, clings to the damp plaster, smothers the faint trace of YSL Paris perfume that still lingers like a rumour on the stairwell. Was that the scent of his daughter, or his wife?

He turns more pancakes carefully carefully, because torn skins spill everything and watches orange filling ooze, then seal, then ooze again.

He remembers sealing other things: sandwiches for school lunches, crusts cut off, layered with tissue the way she loved; his carefully made beef bourguignon slow-braised for Sundays, his home-made garlic bread, the whole house singing with wine and thyme; his homemade soups she swore were magic.

He repeats the motion, flip, hiss, flip, like penance, while the freezer hums behind him, packed the way she left it: frozen chips, frozen peas, frozen days.

Outside, a dog barks once, twice, then falls silent. Inside, silence answers back, louder.

He was unfaithful.

The thought arrives like the drip of the leaking tap: steady, unstoppable. He had grown bored with her sameness; how cruel the word seems now, "sameness" and slipped out to Jade, bright-eyed Jade who still waves in the village as though nothing is secret. *Unfaithful,* the word echoes, softer the second time, striking the walls like a bell struck under water.

He presses two fingers to the bristle of his unshaven chin and feels the roughness penance again, then wipes them on the unused towel draped over the back of a chair.

The towel smells of detergent and neglect. He hasn't washed properly in days. When the hush grows too large, he reaches for the porn magazines hidden beneath the bread bin, thumbs their glossed edges, but even that bright hunger feels moth-eaten now, fluttering, dying desire.

Light slants in from the cloud-shrouded window; grey, thin, surgical. It finds the photograph on the fridge: he and Serafina cutting a birthday cake, her arm looped through his as though they were one creature. Already the colours bleach toward sepia; soon it will fade entirely.

Beside the range an armchair sags, Serafina's armchair, fabric shiny where she once curled with giraffe trinkets on the sill behind her. No one sits there except, on rare afternoons, their daughter; who pulls her knees up and stares at the empty hallway as though expecting her mother to bustle in balancing soup ladle and laughter.

The house feels it too: rafters bowing, windows inhaling their own dust, the smell of sick-sweet cheese drifting upward like a prayer that won't land.

Robert plates the pancakes, watches steam coil, and tells himself, again, that she loved him, worshipped him, called him her rock. Tells himself, again, that accidents happen, that blood does not always mean guilt. Yet the tap drips, the clock limps, and every echo in the hallway sounds like her soft step returning to ask why he was gone so long.

***

**Author's Clinical Notes:**

When I read this chapter now, what strikes me is not him.

It's the architecture.

I had barely met this man, yet I constructed an entire interior world around him; the farmhouse, the mountains, the rootedness, the steadiness, the smell of soup simmering on the stove, the solid wooden table, the deep community ties.

I wasn't describing him.

I was describing what I lacked.

He became a vessel for everything I felt exiled from.

Roots.

Belonging.

Continuity.

Stability.

A father who stayed.

A man who cooked.

A life that did not shift underfoot.

Projection is not stupidity.

Projection is hunger.

When you grow up without solidity, you scan for it like water.

I projected onto him the man who had deep roots because I had none.

The man who belonged where he stood because I never felt installed.

The man who had history in the soil because my history felt severed.

And here is the uncomfortable truth:

Fantasy felt safer than reality.

In fantasy, he was nurturing.

In fantasy, he was emotionally available.

In fantasy, he was solid and chosen and stable.

Reality is unpredictable.

Reality sweats.

Reality disappoints.

Reality ranks.

Fantasy never rejects you.

It waits.

Notice something else.

Even as I built him into a figure of steadiness, I carried the quiet belief that I would ruin it.

That I would become jealous.

That I would interrogate his past.

That I would feel inferior to any woman who had come before me.

That I would scan for signs I was second.

I had already decided I was different.

Different meant defective.

Different meant less real.

Different meant provisional.

Other women felt "normal" to me.

They felt embodied.

Installed.

Legitimate.

I felt spectral.

And if you feel spectral, you assume others will eventually see through you.

So, I developed a strategy:

Leave first.

I always walked away.

Not because I was strong.

Because I was terrified.

I feared rejection so profoundly that I rehearsed it in advance.

If I leave, I cannot be dethroned.

If I leave, I maintain sovereignty.

If I leave, I control the ending.

Control masquerades as independence when you have never felt secure.

And here is another layer.

I preferred my relationships suspended in longing.

Longing is intoxicating.

Longing is safe.

Longing allows you to remain half-formed.

Actual embodied intimacy is riskier.

When bodies meet in reality, you must show up.

You must stay.

You must tolerate being seen.

You must tolerate being chosen, or not.

Sweaty, fleshy reality requires inhabiting yourself.

Fantasy allows you to hover above your own life.

I did not yet understand that my jealousy of other women was not about them.

It was about embodiment.

They seemed rooted.

I felt temporary.

They seemed solid.

I felt floaty.

They seemed to occupy space.

I felt like I was borrowing it.

So, I built a man who symbolised permanence.

And I loved the idea of him.

Because the idea of him did not demand that I fully arrive.

This is not a story about falling in love.

It is a story about trying to graft yourself onto someone else's roots because you are not yet rooted in your own body.

At this point in the narrative, I believed I wanted him.

What I truly wanted was installation. And installation does not come from marrying into someone else's solidity.

It comes from inhabiting your own.

# Chapter Four: Chrissy.

*Sweet William: Named for gallantry, and yet in the old poems, they stand for heartache.*

*

Chrissy stood in the kitchen in bare feet, the tiles cold under her arches. She was rolling meatballs between her palms; slow, almost meditative; as the news flickered soundlessly on the tiny television perched near the kettle.

She stirred the sauce with a wooden spoon, a strand of hair stuck to her cheek, a smear of tomato on her wrist. The scent of garlic and oregano rose like a hymn.

Outside, January clouds had fallen softly, painting the garden grey-blue. Ivy curled in against the glass.

Nadine was due any minute.

Fresh spaghetti boiled. A packet of grated cheese lay unopened. Two glasses sat waiting like old confidantes. Chrissy stared at them, tilted her head, and for a second imagined they were his....hers and his. She shook it off.

He hadn't rung to confirm lunch today.

She hadn't expected him to, not really. It had only been one meeting. One strange meeting in a nightclub. But still, something about the lines of his face had stayed. Something about the voice. The voice especially that low, sandpaper rasp with secrets behind it.

The doorbell rang.

Nadine came in wrapped in an enormous baby pink scarf, smelling of rain and powdery Guerlain's Mitsouko. Her golden-blonde hair was wet and tied up messily, her eyes lined in kohl, a bottle of red in one hand and a tin of Viennese whirls in the other.

"Christ alive, you're doing tomato sauce meatballs. You goddess."

Chrissy laughed. "I had a packet of mince. I'd a need for comfort food."

They settled around the table, wine poured deep, steam curling off bowls. The sauce clung to the pasta just right. Nadine poked at her food with exaggerated reverence.

"Widowers," she said eventually, "are strange things. They haunt themselves. I still set the table for two sometimes. Then I catch myself, get all embarrassed. But who's watching? Me and the ghosts, that's all."

Chrissy smiled softly. "You were in love with your husband very deeply?"

Nadine nodded. "Still am. I still think he's waiting for me in heaven."

They both laughed gently, but the laughter turned inward, private.

"His wife," Chrissy said suddenly. "His name's Robert. His wife was called Serafina. Isn't that an old-fashioned name? Pretty, though."

"Was she beautiful?"

Chrissy paused, then shrugged. "I don't know. I haven't looked her up online. She's only been deceased for six months. I kind of don't want to. I think she was very beautiful. She *feels* beautiful. That's worse somehow. I keep imagining her wearing sage green velvet. Isn't that strange?"

Nadine smiled with tired eyes.

"You've got it bad, haven't you?"

Chrissy rolled her eyes. "He hasn't even fucking rung. We were supposed to go out for lunch today in town. And he was to ring back to get my address; but he hasn't bothered."

"Jesus. I'm sorry! Can't win them all I suppose."

They stayed at the table for hours, music low, red wine warm in their cheeks. At one point, they played songs from the nineties on Nadine's phone, got up and danced in stockinged feet, laughing at how loud their knees cracked. Nadine sang along badly to Everything but

The Girl. Chrissy did the worst version of Groove Is in the Heart ever recorded.

When Nadine left at 7pm, there was the usual flurry of hugs, promises to do it again, the slammed cab door, the retreating lights down the lane.

Chrissy washed up slowly. She spent the evening trying to get clients by making small clips about her therapy service on Tik Tok. It was no good; she was no Teal Swan.

The silence returned.

Upstairs, at 11pm she changed into her nightdress; pale lavender, slightly too soft from too many washes. She brushed her hair, rubbed rose oil into her hands. The old house groaned under the weight of old plumbing and stories that didn't belong to her. The window creaked.

Then, just before midnight, something slammed.

A door?

She froze. *Him?* No, he didn't even know her address. He hadn't rung back. He hadn't come.

Wind curled like fingers around the window frame. She looked out. The trees at the end of the garden were bending slightly. Storm-light flickered on the horizon; not lightning, not quite; just a strange silver-blue haze.

She wrapped her arms around herself, rubbing her own shoulders. It was cold. Colder than it should ever have been. She glanced at her writing desk; the piles of old notebooks, the draft she was meant to be finishing.

The career of psychotherapy, that had begun as bravery and now felt like a child's game. Adventures instead of income. Pieces instead of stability.

She'd never grown up properly, had she?

Other women; the women on TV, the ones with planners and schedules and polite moneyed-up husbands; they were *real.* Chrissy felt like a ghost beside them. Or a schoolgirl. Giggling, always giggling.

Yet, life wasn't a joke, it was full of people who did it all by the manual; the house, the husband, the children; the perfect life, the respect off of the community. If it weren't for them; the rest of us might be able to fuck it up; get it wrong, *fuck them* she thought venomously. Yet, hadn't Robert got it right, children, a wife, a farmhouse. She felt proud of the way he had lived. This stranger.

She lit a candle beside her bed and slid under the duvet. The storm hadn't broken yet, but the air had a texture to it; grainy, sharp.

*Robert.*

She thought of him obsessively and hated herself for it. Of the way he hadn't rung back to get her address to take her for lunch; like they had planned. Of how she had wanted to tell him something she didn't understand.

She closed her eyes.

The last image before sleep took her was velvet. Sage green velvet. A woman's back, turned toward her.

Wind through tall grass.

And a clock ticking far away.

The wind had shifted. Chrissy noticed the chill when she woke and went to the kitchen to get hot milk cocoa; the taste of it, caught in the throat like dust and rust and something else... something softer. Rotten roses. That was the smell. Faint, sour-sweet, like a long-dead bouquet left in the dark corner of a forgotten church.

Windows rattled in their old wooden frames. She shivered as she padded through the kitchen in her ballet pumps, setting the kettle to boil, the house silent except for the huff and sigh of the central heating trying its best. Nadine's laughter still echoing in her ears from earlier.

Nadine had told a story about catching herself whispering to her late husband's photograph, and Chrissy had laughed too hard, the wine melting her spine. But now the silence had settled in again, like dust.

There was no cocoa so she made Horlicks. Sat at the table. Lit a scented violet candle.

And somewhere, faintly, the fog began to slip beneath the back door. Unseen, but felt. A pressure on the chest. The kind of quiet that wraps its fingers around your wrist.

She went back to bed. The same dream came like silk catching on thorns.

She was walking barefoot across the back field. It was dusk or dawn; neither and both. The grass was wet, her hem soaked. And ahead of her stood a woman in a coat of green velvet, heavy with damp. One hand gloved, the other bare. She was turned away, her profile sharp, ice blonde hair pinned with a tortoiseshell comb.

Chrissy tried to speak but her mouth was full of sand. The woman turned. And moved toward her. Not walked; moved. Graceful, yes. But not alive.

There was something hinged in the shoulders, something too smooth in the turn of the neck. She stopped a foot away. Her gloves were ruined, one torn at the fingertips. Her mouth raw. Charred around the lips. Something bubbled beneath her cheek, not quite healed.

Chrissy swallowed. "What happened?"

The woman's eyes were pale, almost grey.

"He'll ring you tomorrow to say he's sorry," she said, calmly. Then, more quietly: "Don't fall in love with my husband."

Chrissy stepped back. The air split like silk tearing on a nail.

"Why?"

"You don't even know him," the woman whispered.

And just like that, they were inside the farmhouse. Chrissy was standing in a small warm kitchen, barefoot on cork tiles, wearing someone else's slippers. A girl was laughing in the other room; a child. There was maple syrup. Fried batter. A man; Robert, standing in the doorway with a cup of coffee.

He looked at her, brows drawn.

"How come you're still here?" he asked.

Chrissy turned. The walls were dark. The light wrong. She'd been here before. She'd dreamed this once; she was sure of it. The woman's voice came again, close to her ear.

"This was all mine. All of it."

Chrissy spun around. But the woman was gone. A breeze swept through the kitchen. Not real: too cold, too still. And the smell: old roses, soaked in sea-salt and smoke.

Behind her, a pair of gloves lay on the counter. One was whole. The other torn, blackened at the fingertips.

Chrissy woke up gasping, the bedsheets damp. Somewhere, outside, the wind had picked up. The house creaked and smelt salty like the sea. She sat up slowly.

The next night, the really icy late January rain arrived. It came in sudden, hissing sheets, sweeping sideways down Botanic Avenue and turning the gutters to dark, rushing rivers.

Chrissy stood under a broken bus shelter, her coat thin, her dress clinging to her thighs, the hem dark with rainwater. She hadn't brought an umbrella. She didn't own one anymore.

Inside the pub; McGuinness's, once a gentleman's club, now full of indie girls and poets pretending to be plumbers; the music was already starting.

The bassline pulsed through the walls like a slow, persistent heart. Somewhere inside, Nadine and Pauline would be holding a corner booth hostage with their handbags and their opinions.

She went in. Steam rose off her as she stepped into the warmth. The scent of beer, damp wool, and pub chips enveloped her like a scratchy old blanket. Her hair stuck to her forehead. She gave a half-smile to the young barman who didn't smile back, and walked slowly, deliberately, towards her friends.

They made space. Nadine had lavender gin. Pauline had red wine. They'd both made an effort; perfume, mascara, scarves. Chrissy had made an effort too, in her own way. A velvet ribbon in her hair. Lipstick, slightly smudged.

The band were tuning up. They were all bones and beards. The singer looked like a mechanic who read Neruda. She sat. She drank. She laughed. She tried.

But even in laughter, she felt the long ache of time.

Around her, couples touched shoulders. A woman in her twenties danced with abandon, her boyfriend beaming at her like she was made of moonlight.

A toddler with enormous eyes clung to his young father near the back, probably a cousin of someone in the band. Chrissy's chest caught. *How did I get so far away from all of this?*

*Time.* Time was running out. For motherhood. For marriage. For the sort of skin-to-skin love that rewrote everything. Her fingers ached with it.

She was just reaching for her wine again when she saw him. At the doorway. Just beyond the crowd. Dark hair. Pale face. Leaning slightly. Watching. Not moving. Those haunted blue eyes with the gold ring like the inside of an old locket.

For one terrible, beautiful second, she thought; he's here. Her body moved before her mind could catch up, standing, pushing past strangers, angling herself toward the doorway. But he was gone.

Only a teenage boy remained, shouldering his way to the bar, wearing a school blazer and acne. Nothing at all like Robert. She sat back down. Her heart, for reasons it could not explain, had begun to pound.

Later, the girls came back to hers. She made them lemon muffins, halfway drunk and still wet from the rain. They talked about men. Nadine said she was too old to start again. Pauline talked about her new hospital position.

Chrissy barely heard. She was staring at her mobile phone. Just staring. Then, when the house was quiet again, when the smell of lemon sugar and rain had gone still in the kitchen, she called him.

It rang. Once. Twice. Three times.

Then:

"Hi."

"It's Christine."

"Hi." His voice like gravel under velvet.

She almost hung up. But her voice came out in a rush:

"Did I see you tonight? At the band? I thought... I don't know."

A pause. Then:

"No. I wasn't there."

A longer pause.

"Look, I'm sorry I didn't ring. I'm sorry about Wednesday."

"No, it's fine honestly,' she heard herself saying.

"I wanted to," he said. "I wanted to see if I could stop thinking about you. But I can't."

She closed her eyes. Rain still fell against the windows.

"It's really ok," she said. "I'm, I'm ok."

He hesitated. "Can we try again to meet for lunch next Thursday?"

She laughed aloud. "Yes. Why not."

She gave him her address. Then the line went dead. She sat in the kitchen long after, holding the phone to her chest. She couldn't feel her numb fingers. The silence of the house rose around her like water.

In the dark beyond the windows, Belfast dripped and whispered and waited. And she knew, somehow, that something was about to change. Not because she wanted it to. But because it already had.

***

**Author's Clinical Notes:**

This chapter is not about a dead wife.

It is about comparison.

Notice how quickly the focus shifts from him to her.

Not Seraphina as a person; Seraphina as symbol.

I barely knew anything about this woman. Yet I constructed her in sage green velvet, luminous, serene, intact. She became an emblem of something I believed I was not.

Beautiful.

Chosen.

Legitimate.

Installed.

It did not matter whether she truly embodied those qualities.

What mattered was what she represented to me.

When you grow up without secure belonging, you do not simply want love.

You want proof.

Proof that you count.

Proof that you are not provisional.

Proof that you are not the second draft.

The widowed wife becomes dangerous not because she is dead; but because she was first.

First wife.

First mother of his children.

First installed woman in his life.

And if you carry a fracture around being chosen and then dethroned, first place matters more than it should.

This is not vanity.

It is existential ranking.

Other women felt "real" to me.

I use that word deliberately.

*Real.*

Women with planners and school runs and husbands and communities. Women whose lives appeared to follow a script. They seemed sanctioned.

I felt improvised.

I had a career, yes; but I treated it like a child's game. I did not inhabit it with authority. I floated around it. I half-claimed it. I half-claimed myself.

I was in my thirties and still felt as if life had not properly begun.

That sensation is profoundly common among women who grew up without solid attachment. There is a chronic delay in the internal clock. You feel developmentally displaced. As if everyone else received a manual.

House.

Husband.

Children.

Community.

The "manual" women seemed grounded. I felt experimental.

And here is the painful truth beneath the venom:

I resented women who looked secure because they mirrored my own fear of illegitimacy.

If belonging was revocable in childhood, you never fully trust that it can be permanent in adulthood.

So, you watch other women for signs of stability.

You rank them.

You rank yourself lower.

You feel counterfeit.

I did not envy Seraphina because she was beautiful.

I envied her because she had been chosen first and lived publicly as his wife.

There is something profoundly stabilising about public installation.

To be someone's wife.

To be someone's mother.

To have photographs in frames.

To have continuity.

Ghosts do not get framed.

And that is what I felt like in my thirties.

A ghost observing women who had been granted solidity.

When I write, "If it weren't for them, the rest of us might be able to fuck it up," there is humour, but there is also despair.

If no one embodied the script successfully, I could relax.

But they did.

And their existence felt like evidence against me.

Notice the self-attack:

"I've never grown up properly, have I?"

This is shame speaking.

When sovereignty fractures early, adulthood feels like theatre. You perform competence. You perform sexuality. You perform independence. But internally, you feel like a child waiting to be found out.

So, when he does not call, the old hierarchy activates:

She was real.

I am provisional.

She was wife.

I am fantasy.

This is not about the man.

This is about installation.

The deeper terror was never that he loved her.

It was that I might never feel fully real in anyone's life.

And that is a brutal position for a woman to occupy.

Because society still measures female legitimacy through attachment; marriage, motherhood, visible belonging.

Even the most independent woman can feel the undertow of that cultural current. I was not grieving him.

I was grieving the version of myself I believed I should already have become. That grief is rarely named. But it sits in many women's kitchens at night.

# Chapter Five: New Beginning.

*Ivy: She clings, not to suffocate, but to remember. Ivy endures where others do not ... a symbol of love's tenacity.*

*

Chrissy poured a glass of wine and carried the wine to the settee in a narrow crystal glass, the colour of garnet. It made her feel faintly decadent, as if she were a character in an old DH Lawrence novel, though she couldn't tell yet whether it was a larky tragedy or a passionate love story.

Something about the sweetness; the clinging berry fruit of the alcohol was a lullaby to her nervous system. A memory of being held. She bought the wine to her lips and opened the novel again: The Shadow of the Wind. The paper smelled of damp paperbacks and forgotten afternoons. She read three pages; something about a man being hunted by the devil, a love that could not be named. Her eyes kept scanning the same sentence:

"Every book, every volume you see here, has a soul."

She curled beneath the thin cashmere throw, the night pressing cold against the old windowpanes.

On her lap was a battered copy of The Shadow of the Wind, pages softened by other people's fingers, a faint scent of pipe smoke lingering on the spine.

She read about haunted souls and forgotten books and men who'd made deals with devils. She paused on a line about memory being a form of resurrection. She closed the book. Laid it on her chest.

Outside, the night's freezing cold wind had picked up. It tapped gently at the windowpanes like a child trying to be let in. She turned off the lamp. The room fell into a soft darkness.

Her mind flicked toward Robert. The man who looked like nobody and everybody. The man who'd seemed stitched from her own past and placed, impossibly, in her present. She was certain she'd seen him again tonight; just for a second by the riverbank, under the amber gaslight. Then the dream took her.

And she dreamed. She was standing in a desert. The air was blue and gold, heat rising off the sand in waves. Her feet were bare. Her thin summery dress clung to her knees. She felt thirsty but not afraid. The hot red sun was enormous above her, hanging low, like a god that had decided not to leave the sky.

Ahead, standing in the heat shimmer, was his dead wife.

Ice blonde, classy, tall, golden freckled, half-smiling like she knew something no one else did. An exquisite silk turquoise scarf fluttered around her neck. Her arms were bare.

"I don't live in your world anymore," she said, with no greeting.

Chrissy wanted to speak, to explain. "I'm meeting your husband," she said, and the words felt strange, foreign, like something borrowed from another language. "For lunch. I think we...."

Serafina stepped forward and touched Chrissy's chest. Not harshly. Not kindly either. Just a gesture.

"Be warned," she said. "Not everything dead is gone."

Chrissy's stomach twisted. A kind of kick, low down, sharp. "Were you both madly in love with each other?" she whispered. "Before...before the end?"

His dead wife didn't answer. She turned, walking away through the sand until the heat swallowed her.

Chrissy was standing in a desert at nightfall. The sand was black as iron filings, and the sky above was vast and bruised, swirling with purples and ancient gold. She glanced down and saw she wore no shoes. The earth beneath her feet was warm.

Serafina came up from behind her and spoke softly, without turning her head. Her voice seemed to come from the air itself, not her lips.

"I want to tell you something silly; something small." Then she turned and reached out her hand.

They were standing inside a forgotten hotel. The wallpaper was pale blue, curling at the edges. Seaweed grew from the corners of the ceiling. The lobby was filled with the faint sound of ballroom music; scratchy, distant, echoing like memory. In the corner stood a cracked mirror, and in it, Chrissy saw movement that didn't match hers.

They walked together past tarnished chandeliers, through dusted velvet corridors, until they reached the grand ballroom. It was filled with dancers, but they moved in slow motion, their faces blurred, their clothing from another era. And at the far end of the room: Robert.

He stood alone, in a charcoal suit, under a flickering gaslight that shouldn't have existed. But he looked different. Not older. Not younger. Just changed. As if something had happened to his soul in the interim. Chrissy's chest ached. Was he broken inside, still? Had he always been?

She tried to call out, but Serafina held her wrist gently.

"Love's not a possession," she said. "It's a wound."

Chrissy turned; but the dream had folded in on itself. The seaweed had curled into letters. The dancers were frozen. Robert began to fade. She woke gasping.

It was 4:17 a.m. The digital clock glowed faint red beside her bed. Rain tapped at the glass, finer now, more like mist. Her sheets were tangled around her waist. Her breath was uneven. She stared at the ceiling and hated that it was so cold.

Her heart beat in the hollow of her throat. How hard it must be, she thought, to begin something with a man who's not only known a mad, passionate love but that love hasn't drifted, or divorced; but ripped apart in the most final of ways ....through death.

Was he broken?

It would make sense.

That low voice, that shadow in his eyes. The way he danced with her like it meant something and then disappeared into the night like a secret being kept from himself.

Chrissy knew that people didn't die. Not really. They shifted dimensions. They crossed over, but they stayed. Especially the ones who had loved and been loved deeply.

She could feel it in her bones. In the edges of the mirror. Serafina had not gone. Somehow, it felt as though he still belonged to her.

And yet love was not ownership. Love was not a leash. It was a letting. A longing. A soft kind of possession that asked for nothing except to be allowed to exist.

Chrissy sat up slowly. Her mug of milky Horlicks was cold now. She drank it anyway.

She got up and went to stare out of the window. A dawn had begun to bloom, pale and silver, brushing the brickwork with ghost-light.

The streets were still empty, slick with rain. Trees trembled. Somewhere a bird was trying out its morning call, haltingly, as if unsure whether to commit to the day.

By lunchtime; by one o'clock he would be here.

The thought sent a cold thrill through her. She wrapped her arms around herself. *Afraid.* Excited. *Afraid.*

What was this? A meeting? An adventure? Or another of life's tricks; the sort that pretends to offer a gift, only to laugh behind your back when you unwrap it?

She'd been tricked before. She'd been laughed at. Sometimes she thought even God didn't like her; hated her guts even; didn't trust her with happiness, or maybe didn't think she deserved it? Life had been so harsh so problematic and she knew other sailed through it like it was an adventure; how she hated them bitterly and felt bad for the hate; it made it somehow even worse.

And yet...What if this was the beginning of the story she'd always dreamed of? The white wedding dress. The church aisle. The candlelit house with children's drawings taped to the fridge.

She hadn't felt this excited about a man in years. Not even a flicker. And now; this electricity, this ache in her fingertips. The memory of a dance and the taste of vodka and coffee liqueur on her tongue.

*Would he look the same?* Would his eyes still be stunning sapphire blue, with the lion-like gold around the dark centre; like flames trapped in ice? Gold like the inside of an antique locket. Would his skin be that same strange pale that made his hair seem like ink, like something written across a page of snow? Or had she conjured him up out of black Russians and loneliness?

She drummed her fingertips against a mug of hot tea.

Hours passed slowly. She spent four hours in the bath, letting the hot water soothe the thoughts that kept spiralling.

She washed her hair twice. She shaved her legs. She perfumed the backs of her knees with the sandalwood and rose scent he'd complimented her on up at the bar in the nightclub.

She lay on her bed wrapped in a towel and must have fallen asleep. Her breath caught. Her body was trembling faintly, as though the dream had left something behind inside her.

She opened her eyes and whispered, "Serafina."

But the room was empty. Her book had fallen to the floor. Her mug sat half-full on the nightstand. The world outside was fogged in mist, cloaked and waiting.

She didn't rise immediately. She lay still, staring at the ceiling, trying to remember the exact shade of Robert's eyes; sapphire blue, but with something gold in the centre, like the sun burning in a cold sea. His hair had been dark. Silken. A painter's black; like ink before it dries.

She boiled water and made coffee, but she forgot to drink it. The mug cooled beside her as she sat at the window and watched the fog wrap itself around the rooftops. New lipstick. She hadn't worn red in years. She found it in the bottom of a drawer, kissed with dust. She twisted the tube slowly and ran the colour along her mouth. It looked too bright, too young. She wiped it away, then applied it again.

Time began to dilate. Time became thick, molasses-slow. She brushed her hair a hundred times. Painted her nails and then stripped the colour off.

She changed her outfit three times. There was something sacred about it all. Every act was an offering. She felt she was being watched not by someone malicious, but by fate itself.

*Was this the start of a story?*

Sometimes life sneered. It turned up again with a punchline and made her believe in dreams just before snatching them away. That's what scared her most; the idea that life didn't love her. Or was this different?

Was this the beginning of something gentle? Something that led to walking up an aisle in ivory lace? To the birth of a son? To the return of her body to warmth and her heart to breath?

The knock came at 1pm.

But she didn't answer.

Not at first.

She ran to the window, heart hammering. If it wasn't him... if it had all been some vodka-tinted delusion, she would crumble. She opened the sash slowly and looked down.

*It was him.*

That beautiful dark hair, too shiny to be real. The contrast of it against his skin. His eyes; sapphire ringed in gold, exactly as they'd been. The dream had not invented him. She hadn't conjured him like a spell. *He was here.*

He looked up. She laughed; just out of sheer happiness.

She opened and leaned out of the window and shouted down, "It's you; it's really you, then."

Robert smiled back up at her; the same heart-breaking smile that undid her soul. And in that moment, she forgot he was a widower. She wanted only the hour ahead. And maybe the next. And maybe all the hours she had left of life.

***

**Author's Clinical Notes:**

This chapter looks like relief.

He calls.

He apologises.

He says he cannot stop thinking about her.

And suddenly the narrative shifts from rejection to pursuit.

But notice something important.

He did not call.

She did.

I broke my own rule.

I had always maintained the illusion of sovereignty by leaving first or waiting to be chosen. But here, I chased.

That matters.

When you fear rejection, you often operate inside rigid rules:

If he wants me, he will call.

If I matter, I will be pursued.

If I chase, I lose value.

These rules are not romantic codes.

They are protection systems.

But something in me overrode it.

Why?

Because longing had crossed into anxiety.

When attachment activates in someone with early instability, waiting becomes intolerable. The nervous system cannot tolerate ambiguity.

So, I called.

And when he said, "I can't stop thinking about you," the relief was disproportionate.

That relief was not about love.

It was about regulation.

Ambiguity had been resolved.

Ambiguity is excruciating when your early life taught you that connection can vanish without warning.

Now notice another layer.

I ask myself, "Is he broken?"

That question is not curiosity.

It is pattern recognition.

I was drawn to men who carried fracture.

Widower.

Intensity.

Shadow.

*Why?*

Because a fully regulated, available man would require me to be fully available too.

A broken man allows partial engagement.

A man with a ghost already in the room allows triangulation.

You never have to stand alone as the sole emotional axis.

It distributes the pressure.

And pressure terrified me.

Also notice the narrative tone.

"Was this the start of a story?"

I was constantly narrating my life instead of living it.

Journalism was not accidental. Narration is a refined form of dissociation. If you turn your life into prose, you can stay slightly above it.

You can aestheticise anxiety.

Romanticise fear.

Transform dread into metaphor.

*It feels safer.*

When he knocks on the door and looks exactly as remembered, the relief is physical.

Attraction confirmed.

Fantasy validated.

But underneath the excitement sits something else:

*Fear.*

Excitement and fear often share the same physiological signature.

In a system wired for instability, love does not feel calm.

It feels activating. Heart racing. Thought spinning. Future projecting. That activation can be mistaken for destiny.

But activation is not necessarily intimacy.

At this stage, I was not asking:

Can I be fully present?

I was asking:

Is this story beginning?

The difference matters.

When you grow up without rootedness, you look for narrative arcs.

*Beginnings.*

*Middles.*

*Endings.*

Because narrative feels like structure.

But relationships are not novels.

They are bodies meeting bodies.

And I was still half-ghost.

So yes, this chapter gives us something vital.

It shows the first crack in the waiting posture.

I pursued.

I stepped forward.

But I did so from activation, not grounded embodiment.

That difference will matter later.

Because excitement without sovereignty can become obsession.

And relief from ambiguity can become dependency.
At this point, I believed something magical was beginning.
In truth, something old was being activated.

# Chapter Six: The First Date.

*Forget-me-not; even in the quietest moments, I will remember you.*

He arrived earlier than she expected.

She saw him first through the glass, standing on the pavement as though he had been placed there rather than having arrived by ordinary means.

Belfast had that pale, rinsed look it sometimes took on, as if the city had been up since dawn and was already tired of itself. The sky was a thin grey sheet, neither promising rain nor withholding it.

He stood with his hands in the pockets of his coat, shoulders slightly hunched, looking at the door with a seriousness that suggested he was preparing himself.

She felt, absurdly, as though she were being observed from the inside.

She had not dressed for him. That was the rule she had made for herself, a small, stubborn one. She had dressed for the day. Wool against her skin, the soft scratch of it reassuring, a colour that held its own without pleading. She had brushed her hair and then stopped, leaving it as it wanted to fall. There was a steadiness to her movements, a refusal to rush toward anything, even as something in her chest had begun to tighten.

When she opened the door, he looked up as though startled by the confirmation that she was real.

"Hello," he said.

"Hello," she answered.

They stood like that for a moment, the ordinary space between two people who had spoken already but had not yet been near each other.

His face was thinner than she had imagined, the planes of it sharpened by a kind of restraint.

He had the look of a man who had learned to keep things inside. His eyes moved quickly, taking in the hallway behind her, the light, the domestic quiet. Something flickered there, not longing exactly, but recognition.

"You're right on time," she said, and then realised he was early.

"I didn't want to be late," he said. "I drove down this morning."

From Tyrone, she thought. From that farmhouse with its fields and its silences. From the place where his wife had lived and died.

She took her coat and bag and locked the door behind her. The click of the lock felt decisive, ceremonial even, and she was aware of her body crossing a small threshold.

Outside, the air was colder than she had expected, carrying the faint smell of damp stone and traffic.

"How was the drive?" she asked.

"Long," he said. "Quiet."

He smiled then, briefly, as though apologising for the word. Quiet was his natural language now, she sensed, not something he had chosen but something that had settled on him.

They talked about the road, the weather, the slowness of the morning traffic. He spoke in complete sentences, carefully weighted, and she noticed that he did not fill the gaps when she let silence appear. He seemed content to walk alongside it.

"You look exactly as I imagined," he said.

"That's dangerous," she replied lightly. "Imagination has a lot to answer for."

He nodded. "I know."

There it was, the first small admission, offered without drama. She felt it land and settle. He did not reach for her. He did not tell her anything unnecessary. Instead, he spoke about his children, carefully, naming their ages, their habits, the way the house changed when they were there and when they were not. He spoke of the land, the work that needed doing even in winter, the way animals anchored time.

"And your wife?" she asked, gently, not because she wanted the story but because the space had opened for it.

He did not flinch.

"Serafina," he said, and said the name as though it were still warm in his mouth. "She died last summer."

"I'm so sorry," she said.

"Yes," he answered, and there was no self-pity in it, only fact.

As he spoke, she noticed something strange and unsettling. He did not describe Serafina as absent. He described her as elsewhere. In the corners of rooms, in the habits of the day, in the way light fell across the fields. It was not grief as rupture. It was grief as continuation.

She felt a faint tightening behind her eyes, a pressure she did not acknowledge.

Outside, the sky darkened a shade, the afternoon moving on.

At some point, his hand brushed hers.

It was nothing. It was unmistakable.

Neither of them withdrew immediately. She felt the warmth of his skin, the slight roughness, the living fact of him. Something in her responded, a low recognition that had nothing to do with thought.

They stood outside, the door closing behind them with a muted thud. The street felt louder now, more insistent. He looked at her, and for a moment she thought he might say something reckless or tender or foolish.

He had a blue car.

She noticed it immediately, not because it was remarkable but because it carried a detail that snagged the eye and refused to let go. The number plate ended in 666.

She paused, keys in her hand, the garage door half-raised, and felt the small flicker of amusement and unease that comes when symbolism announces itself without invitation.

"666; that's... ominous," she said, smiling despite herself. "Is that evil, then?"

He laughed, a quick, boyish sound that softened his face. "I've never noticed," he said, though she thought he probably had.

There was something shy between them already, a charge that hadn't yet found its language.

"Shall we take my car?" she asked.

She felt a quiet, irrational pride as she opened the garage and the light fell across the soft curves of the Lotus.

The silvery paint caught the day, glossy and alive, and the interior smelled faintly of leather and something metallic and clean. She had bought it years ago, back when Fleet Street had been her proving ground, when she had needed speed and precision to feel herself fully present in the world. The car still carried that energy. It had not been dulled by time.

He looked at it with open admiration.

"Well," he said. "That changes things."

They drove into town with the roof down, the air cold enough to sting but not enough to hurt. Belfast passed around them in familiar fragments: stone buildings damp with age, traffic lights blinking their patient signals, the smell of diesel and rain and coffee drifting from open doors.

She was acutely aware of her body as she drove, the responsiveness of the car, the way it seemed to listen to her hands. He sat beside her, close but not touching, his presence heavy and contained.

He suggested an upstairs restaurant he knew, somewhere discreet. Thai, she thought later, or something close to it. Warm food. Spices. A room above the street where the noise softened into a distant hum.

Inside, the air was rich with lemongrass and chilli and frying oil. Heat bloomed against her skin as they climbed the stairs. The restaurant was dimmer than the street below, the light golden and forgiving.

They were shown to a table and then, unexpectedly, to a small settee beside it, close enough that their knees brushed when they sat.

She ordered a martini. Dry, or maybe dirty. She couldn't quite remember later which it was, only the sharpness of it, the way the first sip cleared a space behind her eyes.

They talked.

About his children, Kira, Jon, their ages, the way they moved through the farmhouse like weather systems, altering the atmosphere without trying. About Ireland, the fields, the silence, the work that needed doing whether one felt up to it or not. About Belfast, and her life there, the rhythms she had made for herself.

"And your wife; was it sudden?" she asked, when the moment opened and did not feel like a trap.

"Serafina," he said.

The name landed between them with a particular weight, musical and final. He spoke of her without drama, but not without presence. She was not gone in the way one might hope for neatness. She lingered, not as a ghost exactly, but as an organising principle. The way he spoke made it clear that death had not ended the marriage so much as altered its terms.

She listened, aware of something tightening and loosening in her chest at the same time. Women know this feeling. The simultaneous pull of empathy and warning. The question forming even as it is not yet allowed to be asked: Will it be okay?

At some point, they shifted on the settee, closer now, their shoulders touching. The rice arrived, steam rising, white and fragrant. She noticed the way he ate, slowly, deliberately, as though meals had once been rushed and were no longer allowed to be. She noticed the weight of him beside her, the solidity of his presence. There was nothing flimsy about him. Nothing performative. He had a gravity that other men lacked, and she felt herself responding to it with a corresponding softening, a sense of being allowed into her own femininity without effort.

They drank. They talked. Time lost its sharp edges.

At the door afterward, the world rushed back in: the street noise, the cool air, the awareness of being visible again. She invited him up.

In her front room; he stepped closer, and they kissed, briefly at first, and then again, longer, the settee pressing against the backs of her legs as she leaned into him. There was a moment; dangerous, delicious; when it tipped toward something easier, cheaper, the kind of intimacy that collapses into haste.

She pushed him back gently but firmly.

"No," she said, breathless, smiling. "Stop. We can't do this."

He stilled immediately. There was no protest, no sulk, no attempt to reclaim ground. He looked at her with something like relief.

"You're right," he said.

She realised then how much she liked him. How easily this could become something she would later regret if it were not handled with care. She wanted it to be expensive, in the best sense of the word. Earned. Weighted.

There's nothing about you I don't like, she thought, surprised by the clarity of it. The thought arrived whole, unarguable. His brooding, his maleness, the way he seemed to occupy space without needing to announce himself. Other men had failed her because they were too light, too eager to be reassured. He did not ask to be held up.

Instead, he said, "Thank you."

"No, thank you for lunch it was lovely!"

He smiled at her. "I mean, for today; you've come like a ray of sun into something quite dark."

She nodded. He leaned in then and they kissed.

She felt the heat and the chemistry in the kiss and almost breathless as her entire body reacted and wouldn't it be just so easy to pull him inside and have him plunge into her hips; but she wanted him for far more than just that. This was serious.

She watched him walk away, his shoulders slightly hunched against the cold, and felt herself sway, just a little, as though the ground had shifted beneath her. Only when he had got into his blue car and driven off did she realise that her hands were trembling.

After she bought her car in and closed the garage door, the quiet of the house rushed toward her.

In the kitchen, she stood for a moment, not knowing what to do next. Ring a friend. Pour a drink. Sit down. The ordinary options felt suddenly inadequate.

There was excitement, yes; a fizzing, adolescent brightness; but braided tightly with something darker.

Danger, perhaps. Or the knowledge that something had begun that would not be easily unbegun.

When the door closed behind her, she knew it.

Something had started.

That night, she dreamed of a woman standing at the edge of a field, her dress moving in the wind.

***

**Author's Clinical Notes:**

This is the moment where fantasy becomes flesh.

And notice what happens immediately.

I see him through glass. There is always glass.

Observation before contact.

Distance before presence.

Even in this first meeting, I frame him as cinematic; "placed there rather than having arrived by ordinary means." That is myth overlay.

When you aestheticise someone, you avoid meeting them as human.

Humans disappoint.

Myth does not.

Notice also how careful I am not to overdress.

This is not modesty.

This is calibration.

When you have learned that embodiment can trigger intrusion, you regulate how visible you are.

Too much radiance can feel unsafe.

Too little can feel invisible.

So, you aim for controlled attractiveness.

Then he says, "You look exactly as I imagined."

That sentence lands heavily. To be imagined by someone is both flattering and dangerous.

If you are someone who has felt unreal, being imagined can feel like installation. But it also carries risk.

What if you do not match the fantasy?

What if he withdraws once the real you appears?

So, I reply lightly; "Imagination has a lot to answer for."

Humour as deflection.

Charm as shield.

Now look at the control dynamic.

I bring the Lotus.

I drive with the roof down.

I show him my world.

I talk about my work.

That is not arrogance.

That is positioning.

When attraction activates, I instinctively reach for *power.*

If I feel desired, I must not feel owned.
So, I balance desire with status.
Sexual charge plus visible independence.
That combination made me feel sovereign.
Or what I believed sovereignty was at the time.
Now the darker flicker.
When he says his wife "just keeled over," my mind jumps to murder.
*Drama.*
*Danger.*
*Film.*
This is important.
Excitement and suspicion co-exist.
Part of me finds the possibility thrilling.
*Why?*
Because intensity feels familiar.
Calm love had never been my baseline.
Intensity had.
This is the nervous system confusing activation with aliveness.
If there is danger, the story matters.
If there is mystery, I feel engaged.
A stable explanation feels flat.
A dramatic one feels alive.
But this is not romance.
It is trauma patterning.
Now the kiss.
*Deep.*
*Passionate.*
*Mutual.*
And here's the key line:
"I felt I had control because of that."
That is revealing.
Control through sexuality.

*If he desires me strongly, I am not provisional.*

*If he kisses me deeply, I am chosen.*

*If I feel the charge, I am real.*

Sexual attraction becomes evidence of existence.

This is where embodiment and performance blur.

I am present.

But I am also measuring.

Am I wanted enough?

Is the charge strong enough?

Do I hold the upper hand?

When sovereignty fractures early, control often substitutes for safety.

I did not yet understand the difference between:

Being in control

and

Being at ease.

The date ends.

He drives away.

And I interpret it as something having begun.

But what has actually begun is activation.

*Attraction.*

*Projection.*

*Power calibration.*

*Narrative layering.*

Real intimacy has not yet started.

We are still in voltage.

And voltage is seductive.

# Chapter Seven: After the Date:

*White Stock: In floriography, stock means 'you will always be beautiful to me.' A message pressed quietly into petals.*

The date had gone well; into town and a restaurant and then back here and a snog where she'd found it hard to push him off and say, 'Let's save it.'

It had gone well. Not only well but she fancied him so deeply! He was so dreamy; so raw and real and manly. She felt almost dizzy.

Surely this was it! The man who was going to sweep her off her feet. The one she would actually *want* to marry not just feel trapped and claustrophobic when the man mentioned it as she had in the past.

She knew it was far too soon for her mind to go off on such tangents but after so long feeling lukewarm about her dates – to feel so excited about a man felt so refreshing.

The cursor blinks unseen while Chrissy's mind writes its own chapter: Robert. Dark hair, pale skin, those sapphire-blue irises ringed with gold sparks; like a night sky that still remembers noon.

She can almost hear his voice again, that border-country lilt balanced somewhere between Tyrone's granite and Donegal's sea-spray; every vowel seems mapped to winding lanes, to the glens where the moss creeps over stone walls and the streams talk in silver.

She lifts the thin wine glass; still half-full, still trembling and sets it on the mantel beside the tarot deck. Let objects speak: the cards fan open by themselves, as though fate heard its cue. The Lovers card lies face-up. Under its bright stare the whole room tilts toward sunlight. The single cushion suddenly looks expectant, the lone vase purposeful, the dusty giraffe ornament downright whimsical.

The apartment smelled faintly of last night's coffee and old paper, the quiet comforting in a way that was both grounding and sharp.

She poured herself another glass of wine, watching the liquid catch the light, ruby against the pale linen of the kitchen table.

Sitting down, she leaned back and felt the tension in her shoulders unwind just slightly, though not entirely.

Something inside her had shifted. The date had gone well, far better than she had expected. Yet she could feel a thin, metallic edge of herself pressing against the warmth of the evening, a sharpness she could not fully ignore.

It was not jealousy exactly. Not yet. It was the memory of Serafina, hovering in the corners of the room, in his words, in the careful ways he spoke of her. She had felt it as soon as she had opened the door to the restaurant, the awareness that she was stepping into a space that had already been inhabited by love.

It made her wonder, fleetingly, about softer women, women who could cradle grief without it turning into a subtle challenge or a threat. That softness was not her. She had been shaped elsewhere: high streets of ambition, deadlines, the faintly pungent perfume of Fleet Street offices, the smell of ink, the tang of adrenaline in her own veins. She carried that steel still, even now, coiled lightly beneath her skin.

Yet there had been physical attraction, undeniable and fizzing like some dangerous chemical between them. She felt it again now, curling through her chest and down into her belly, making her pulse rise despite the quiet of her flat.

She thought of the way he had leaned closer on the settee, the heat of his shoulder against hers, the way his hand had brushed just so against hers. A small shiver ran through her as she let the memory pool across her body, softening her edges, melting some of that Fleet Street steel still coiled beneath her skin.

She leaned back in her chair, tilting her head, letting her eyes wander to the typewriter on the desk across the room.

## THE PSYCHOLOGY OF FEAR OF LOVE

A blank page stared back at her. The cursor blinked rhythmically, indifferent to her thoughts. She thought of the novel she was working on, the words she still had to coax into the world, and a part of her wondered if writing would ever capture this, this tension, this thrill, this dangerous intersection of desire and fear.

Her gaze drifted to the mirror beside the window, catching the dim reflection of her own face. She traced the line of her jaw with her eyes, the curve of her neck, the way her hair fell in loose waves that she had not bothered to tame.

There was a rawness in her appearance that matched the rawness of her thoughts. The life she had built, rented house, sports car, career, independence, had shaped her into someone formidable, someone who could rise and rise and rise, she thought, but someone who had not yet learned the art of letting herself soften completely.

She poured herself another sip of wine, letting the liquid warm the metallic edge that ran through her chest and fingers. That edge had served her well in the past, had propelled her to the things she had achieved, but tonight it made her question herself.

What if it made her miss something real? What if her sharpness, her ability to measure, to calculate, to dominate, prevented her from surrendering to what might be extraordinary?

And then her thoughts turned back to him, to Robert. She felt herself remembering every detail, the blue of his car, the way the number plate ended in 666, the shy laugh when she had teased him about it, the warmth and weight of his presence beside her, the deliberate way he had eaten, the subtle gravity of him that drew her in.

She wondered if he knew how dangerous it was to be near her, a woman who could melt, yet was capable of cutting, a woman whose ambition ran like molten metal beneath her skin.

Her mind twisted inward, circling the memory of Serafina. Was there still a flame? Even a faint one? She tried to convince herself that it was impossible, that Serafina was gone, six months dead, but the thought lodged itself stubbornly.

What if she had not been entirely extinguished? What if the candle still flickered, if even a memory of her made him pause, made him hesitate, made him see her, this new woman, differently?

She sighed, leaning her head against the cool glass of the window. Outside, the city was muted and restless. Car lights streaked across wet pavements. Rain threatened to fall.

Inside, she felt her pulse in her throat, in the tips of her fingers, a pulse that spoke of anticipation, of caution, of recognition that she had entered into something she could not steer entirely. She had not lost herself in it, not yet, but she knew that physical chemistry, combined with the mental alignment that came so easily between them, meant she was no longer fully in control.

Her hand drifted to the typewriter again, pressing lightly against the keys, imagining sentences that could capture this blur of excitement, fear, and raw desire. But the words were stubborn, only half-formed. She leaned back, swirling her wine again, tasting the subtle bite, feeling the warmth spread through her chest. She could almost forgive herself for the arrogance she had carried that night, the jealousy she had briefly felt, the sharpness that kept her from fully yielding. Almost.

She moved toward her vanity, running her fingers across the bottles of makeup, the brush of powder, the line of lipstick. She traced her collarbone, the edge of her neck, the slope of her shoulders. She smoothed hair over her ears, adjusted it softly, almost unconsciously. Each movement tethered her to herself even as her mind swirled freely with him, the possibility of him, and the dangerous thrill of what might come.

Sitting back, she crossed one leg over the other, tracing patterns on the table with her fingertip. The apartment smelled faintly of paper and polish, wine and rain, and herself, sweat, perfume, memory.

She considered calling a friend, seeking reassurance, or perhaps simply speaking aloud to break the tension coiled inside her chest. She did not. Instead, she let herself sit, let herself feel, let herself reckon with the dizzying mix of desire, fear, ambition, and wonder. Every thought, every shiver, every heartbeat was a reminder that this was new, raw, and alive. That she was alive.

She returned to the typewriter, letting her fingers hover above the keys, imagining letters forming, imagining the tension distilled into words. She tapped a finger lightly, listening to the hollow echo, feeling it resonate through her bones.

Outside, the first drops of rain hit the window, soft, precise. Inside, she felt the soft pull of anticipation, the edge of longing, the thrill of possibility.

She swirled the wine in her glass again, letting it catch the light. Tiny beads clung to the rim, refracting the dim glow from the kitchen. She watched them slowly drip back, hypnotic, like seconds slipping by, and felt her fingers tingle where they rested on the stem.

The warmth pooled in her chest, spreading to her shoulders, softening the tension in her jaw. She exhaled, a slow hiss, and pressed her fingertips lightly against her temples.

Her eyes wandered to the mirror once more. She leaned forward, brushing stray strands of hair behind her ear. The reflection staring back was her, but slightly altered, flushed, alive, edges softened just a fraction by the thrill of the evening.

Her lips parted unconsciously, and she caught herself studying the curve of her neck, the faint line of her collarbone under the soft fall of her shirt. A shiver of awareness ran down her spine.

She reached for her makeup compact, just to occupy her hands. The cool metal pressed against her fingers as she opened it, revealing the smooth powders she had chosen so carefully that morning.

She touched the surface lightly, brushing it against her cheek. The scent of pressed powder mixed with her perfume and the faint trace of wine. It was intimate, grounding, a small act that reminded her of herself while her mind roamed freely.

Her fingers lingered in her hair. She tugged gently, rearranging, twisting, letting it fall in waves again. Every movement felt charged, each touch a tiny acknowledgment of her body's memory of him.

She imagined the brush of his hand, the warmth of his skin against hers, the tilt of his head as he looked at her, slow and unhurried. She felt the pull again, the fizzing chemistry, the impossibility of controlling every spark that flared between them.

She sat back on the chair, letting one leg drape over the other. Her foot tapped lightly against the floor, a quiet rhythm that mirrored her heartbeat. She traced invisible lines on the table with her fingertip, the grain of the wood rough yet familiar beneath her touch.

Outside, the city hummed softly, distant traffic, rain beginning to patter lightly on the pavements, but inside, every sensation was magnified. The wine, the soft hum of the refrigerator, the faint tick of the wall clock, the warmth of her sweater against her skin, all stitched together into a fabric of awareness that made her feel simultaneously alive and fragile.

Her eyes fell to the typewriter again. The cursor blinked, patient, unjudging. She imagined sentences forming, imagined spilling herself onto the page, shaping the tension, the desire, the fear, the exhilaration into words. Her hands hovered above the keys. She flexed her fingers, feeling the subtle strength in them, the memory of typing fast in days past, chasing deadlines, chasing stories, chasing herself.

The thought made her smile faintly. Even now, the rhythm of creation called to her, intertwined with the rhythm of her pulse, the rhythm of the evening, the rhythm of a body remembering something it had not yet fully allowed itself to feel.

She sipped the wine again, the liquid warm and sharp, sliding smoothly down her throat. The scent of the glass, the faint sweetness, the depth of colour in the wine, all of it made her aware of the fine line between indulgence and discipline, between pleasure and control.

She lingered on the memory of him: the settee, the rice, the slight press of his shoulder, the playful shyness in his laugh, the gravity of his presence that contrasted so sharply with her own sharp edges.

Her thoughts spiralled; would he measure up to the journey she envisioned for herself? Could he handle the heights she intended to climb, the intensity she carried, the speed with which her life moved? And yet, there was the pull of the physical, the fizzing chemistry, the impossibility of controlling every spark that flared between them.

She imagined herself melting into that pull, letting herself be carried, letting herself feel, and it terrified her.

She stood, stretching lightly, her body catching the last shimmer of twilight through the window.

She traced the contours of her arms, the soft curve of her shoulders, the line of her neck. She caught herself tilting her head, looking at the reflection again, smiling faintly at the woman who was sharp, ambitious, slightly arrogant, yet fluttering now with possibility.

She pressed her fingertips against her chest, feeling her heartbeat, feeling the pull, the tension, the desire, the fear all coiled together inside her.

Her hand went to the mirror again, brushing her lips with her fingers, checking the faint smudge of lipstick. She adjusted her hair once more, smoothing it, running her fingers through it, letting the waves fall where they pleased.

She inhaled slowly, the scent of her perfume mingling with the wine, the faint hum of the city, the evening air pressing gently through the slightly open window.

For a moment, she considered calling a friend, speaking aloud to break the quiet that felt almost electric. But she did not. Instead, she allowed herself to sit, let herself feel, let herself reckon with the dizzying mix of excitement, fear, desire, and wonder. Every thought, every shiver, every heartbeat was a reminder that this was new, raw, and alive. That she was alive.

She returned to the typewriter, letting her fingers hover above the keys, imagining letters forming, imagining the tension distilled into words. She tapped a finger lightly, listening to the hollow echo, feeling it resonate through her bones.

Outside, the first drops of rain hit the window, soft, precise. Inside, she felt the soft pull of anticipation, the edge of longing, the thrill of possibility.

She leaned back once more, glass in hand, and allowed herself a small, secret smile.

She hadn't used her golden vibrator in ages but she pulled it out of its velvet case and began to warm it up by buzzing it softly against her clitoris. Her body immediately warmed with a surge of heat. Her legs fell open and she unbuttoned her top and began to pull and tug at her own nipples. They hardened immediately as she imagined his head firmly between her legs, his sharp teeth far too close to her delicate folds. She wanted him to rape her, his hardness to destroy her. As she plunged the vibrator inside her she moaned loudly as her mind and body were washed away on an explosion of ecstasy.

This night, this evening, this unexpected pull, it could change everything. And yet, it left her fully herself: sharp, alive, slightly trembling, aware of every nuance, every shade of sensation, every memory and possibility. And in that awareness, she felt the quiet thrill of something she could not yet name but knew she would never forget.

She left the flat with her wine glass emptied and a small buzz still lingering in her chest. The city smelled of damp stone and night air, the faint tang of fried food from a nearby takeaway drifting lazily across the street. She walked quickly, letting the rhythm of her steps match the pulse in her temples, imagining the way she would describe him to someone else without sounding absurdly infatuated.

She knew one person would understand. Nadine.

The café was warm and fragrant with roasted coffee, pastries, and the faint sweetness of syrupy custard tarts tucked in glass domes. She spotted Nadine at a corner table, sunlight slanting over the polished wood, highlighting the strands of gold in her hair, the casual chic of her blouse and scarf. Pauline arrived moments later, jangling keys and smiling, the aroma of her peach perfume mixing with the warm café air.

The three of them settled in, menus forgotten almost immediately, conversation taking off where it always did: fast, intimate, teasing.

She felt a little flutter in her stomach as she sat down, remembering the date, remembering Robert, remembering the pull of him against her skin. Nadine leaned in immediately, eyes sparkling, and asked, "So? How was he? Tell me everything. Was he a good shag?"

She laughed softly, stirring her coffee absentmindedly, the bitter aroma curling up to her nose. "He's... complicated. Charming. Dangerous in ways I can't quite measure. And infuriatingly normal at the same time. Like you wouldn't expect it from someone who has that... gravity."

She waved a hand vaguely, and Nadine tilted her head, attentive.

Pauline smirked. "Gravity? Is this a dating app description or real life?"

"It's real life," she said, though the words themselves made her blush slightly. "He's got this weight, this presence. He makes you want to laugh and roll your eyes at the same time. And the touch... it's ridiculous, really." She lowered her voice, leaning in conspiratorially, the café feeling intimate despite the chatter around them.

Nadine's eyes sparkled. "You're giddy. And here I thought you were supposed to be cool and analytical about all this. What happened?"

She sipped her coffee, tasting the dark roast and the faint hint of cinnamon from the sprinkle on top. "We kissed. And then we had to pull back because I realized I liked him more than I expected. And he... he's just... well, he's a body like a Greek God." She laughed softly, a little embarrassed by the candour, but unable to stop herself. "I can't quite articulate it. I feel like a schoolgirl and a lusty teenager all at once."

Pauline leaned back, grinning, swirling her latte. "Welcome to the human condition. You can be both. It's allowed. But tell me, does he have flaws?"

"Of course," she said, sipping her coffee and letting her eyes drift to the window, catching the reflection of the rainy streets. "Everyone has flaws. He's... intense. Not always aware of how others feel, perhaps. But then again, that intensity is part of it. I can't explain it. I've never... felt like this before."

Nadine reached over and nudged her lightly. "Sounds dangerously close to erotic obsession."

She laughed again, the warmth of friendship, caffeine, and memory mixing in her chest. "It's not sexual obsession. Just... recognition, I think. Something primal. Something that makes you forget time and space for a moment. Something you can't calculate or control."

The conversation drifted then to lighter topics, laughter punctuating each sentence. They compared outfits for upcoming events, speculated on mutual acquaintances, shared small humiliations from the week. But her mind kept returning, like a tide, to him; to the tilt of his head, the soft shyness, the brush of his hand, the way his hard body had made her pulse skip.

She caught herself smiling at a memory she had barely told Nadine, the way he had laughed when she mentioned the number plate on his car, and the way she had felt both proud and ridiculous opening the garage to show off her Lotus.

She realised she'd been holding her breath for much of the day, and now that it was out in conversation, she could feel herself settling, relaxing slightly into the warmth of the café, the friendship, the shared confidences.

Pauline leaned over, lowering her voice. "So, when do we get the next bonk-buster chapter? You going to see him again?"

She shrugged lightly, stirring her coffee. "I don't know. But I want to. I want to see how this... unfolds. And I'm scared too. That's part of it."

The café seemed to close around them, the chatter dimming, the clink of cups softened by the hum of their conversation. She felt a curious thrill; part anticipation, part fear, part lust.

She was living something delicate, ephemeral, intense, and entirely her own. And in that moment, she allowed herself to just be, sipping coffee, feeling the smooth warmth of the cup in her hands, the soft hum of life around her, and the pulse of something new with vibrant colours beginning to stir.

She left the café feeling lighter, the tension of the day now tempered by laughter and confidences shared with Nadine and Pauline.

Outside, the streets glistened with rain, reflecting the late afternoon lights in soft streaks across the pavements. The air smelled faintly of wet stone and the warmth of bakery ovens drifting from nearby shops. Her senses felt more alive and yet softened. She knew that it was him doing this to her and the knowledge both scared and thrilled her.

She tucked her woolly striped scarf closer, and the three of them set off down the street, shoes clicking on cobblestones, voices rising and falling with shared jokes and knowing glances.

Their first stop was a privately owned niche boutique she'd been meaning to visit for weeks. Designer handbags lined the shelves in neat rows, each one polished, each one whispering a promise of elegance and power.

She ran her fingers along the smooth soft leather of a deep burgundy bag, feeling the supple texture, the faint scent of polish and new leather. Nadine held up a small blue velvet clutch, holding it under her chin, modelling it as if on a catwalk, while Pauline twirled in the aisle, laughing at their reflections in the mirrored wall.

She smiled, letting herself be caught up in it, but a small, sharp prickle of unease crept in. Robert.

She imagined him seeing her here, imagining her laughter, imagining the way her hair caught the light in the mirror. And then a flash of jealousy, inexplicable and irrational, at the memory of Serafina, at the invisible presence she seemed to cast over everything.

Why did she have to feel it so sharply? She shook her head slightly, laughing as Nadine held up a teal handbag.

"Oh, this is perfect for you," Nadine said, handing it over. She accepted it, pressing it against her chest, feeling the smooth leather warm under her fingers, and tried to shake off the tiny shadow of unease.

They wandered into the organic cosmetics shop, the air scented with powder, floral perfume, and a subtle sweetness like jasmine that made her think of summer evenings. They examined red lipsticks, swirling them across the back of their hands to test shades, layering coffee coloured blush and green eyeshadow carefully, gossiping about friends, men, and the absurdity of dating in a city that never paused for breath.

She let herself smile, let herself enjoy, and yet even here, in this bright, perfumed world, Robert lingered at the edges of her mind. She imagined his glance, the faint curve of his smile, the way he had tilted his head that night.

Pauline leaned in, whispering conspiratorially. "So, what's he like in bed?" she asked with a mischievous grin, and Nadine elbowed her lightly, eyes twinkling.

She flushed, laughing, covering her mouth with one hand. "I told you! We haven't... we're not there yet," she said, though the memory of that night pressed warmly against her, making her pulse quicken even as she tried to keep it in check.

"And what about the dead wife?" Nadine asked softly, a sudden seriousness threading through her tone. "Do you think he's... still tied to her memory? Their lovemaking, their passion!"

She paused, lips parting, staring at a row of coral-coloured lipsticks as if seeking the answer in their bright, smooth surfaces.

"I don't know," she admitted finally. "I think he's over her, but you never know with memory, with grief. Six months isn't that long."

The words sounded fragile even to her own ears. The musty perfume of the shop, the warmth of the air, the faint buzz of other shoppers all seemed to amplify the uncertainty coiling inside her.

They laughed again, trying to dispel the momentary heaviness. She chose a deep, warm red lipstick, imagining how it would catch the light in candlelit rooms, how it might appear in reflections. Nadine picked a soft pink, Pauline a golden coral, and they stood side by side, testing shades, making faces, leaning close to mirrors, feeling alive and conspicuous all at once.

She found herself thinking about Robert as she sensuously smudged the lipstick over her lips, imagining how he would notice the shade, the way it complimented the curve of her smile.

And then she shook her head slightly, chastising herself for letting him take up so much space in her mind while she wandered the aisles of frivolity and colour. Yet, she could not resist the pull, the memory of warmth, the lightness of laughter tempered by the deep, ache of tension that still lingered in her chest.

As they left the shop, Nadine twirled the bags on her arm, Pauline swinging a new scarf, and she felt herself flushed, exhilarated, alive. The streets glimmered, rain falling lightly, mixing with the scents of bread, new perfume, and wet stone.

She felt a strange dizziness, a mixture of delight and anxiety, and realised that she could not entirely untangle herself from thoughts of him and her growing fear of his dead wife.

Walking past a café window, she caught her pale reflection, hair slightly tousled, lips deep red, eyes bright with apprehension. She pressed her hand to the glass lightly, as if to steady herself, feeling the warmth of the leather handbag under her fingers, the cool rush of air against her cheek.

Somewhere in the depths of her mind, Serafina lingered, quiet and unremarkable to anyone else, but impossible to ignore. And yet, Robert existed in the same breath, vivid and immediate, a force she could not resist.

They paused briefly at a cross street, Nadine chatting animatedly about a mutual friend, Pauline laughing at a joke, and she let herself smile fully, letting the warmth of friendship cushion the edge of her anticipation, the pull of desire, the painful obsessive sting of jealousy.

She realised as she did every time she thought of him, that she was both exhilarated and terrified, that she wanted to lose herself yet feared doing so entirely.

The three of them continued down the street, weaving through light rain, into the warm glow of another shop, voices low and laughing, minds alive, hearts lightly tethered between caution and reckless delight. And through it all, she carried the memory of him, the thrill, the chemistry, the impossibility of control, letting it bloom quietly inside her as she immersed herself in the colours scents, textures, and laughter of a city that seemed to pulse in time with her heartbeat.

I haven't missed the boat for marriage; she joyfully tells the bare walls back at her flat. It's just been idling at the quay, waiting.

A new fire in the grate flares, gold on her shins, and hope rushes in like warm breath. She steps to the mirror and yanks off her clothes and stares; her underwear; white silk and lace bites at her waist, no longer ridicule but promise. She knots her hair high; quick twist, two pins and the reflection blurs into another woman walking down a church aisle, white satin flaring, Robert's steady hands cupping hers.

## THE PSYCHOLOGY OF FEAR OF LOVE

She spritzes the last of her Chanel No. 5 into the air, two pulses, soft rain and moves through it; for the first time in forever the perfume feels earned. Her lips next; deep rose, a colour that expects to be kissed.

Two children, she thinks, dark-blonde with slanting blue eyes, strong hands for building forts, poetic hearts for writing secret songs.

She sees their future house fattening with noise: toy cars under the sofa, Robert's muddy boots at the door, mashed potatoes whipped smooth in a pot while home-made chicken gravy sighs on the hob. The microwave's dull hum is replaced by real simmer, real steam.

Singleness; singleness, singleness: the shame-word rings once, then dissolves in the new refrain together. *Together, together, together.*

She leans closer to the mirror, smiling at this bright-eyed bride-to-be and catches a phantom just behind her shoulder. Blonde hair in a neat bun. A gentler curve of cheek.

*Serafina.*

The name slides between Chrissy's ribs. Widower, he'd said, sapphire eyes darkening. Wife dead only six months. Serafina's coat still on the nail, her picture still on the fridge, her babies already grown.

Chrissy's smile falters; the room contracts. The sunlight thins, turns surgical, then cools to pewter.

In the mirror the high bun looks stolen. She loosens it, but the pins clatter like bones. The Lovers card has flipped; now shows the pale blank of its reverse.

Perfume hangs too heavy, a sweet-sick hospital of flowers. She imagines Robert's hands around Serafina's waist under orchard blossoms; imagines those same hands on her naked, perfect breasts flicking her nipples, taking them into her mouth and madly, deliciously in love. Was it deepest grief she had seen glinting in his gold-flecked eyes over dinner?

Children with slanted blue eyes fade into smoke. The vase, cushion, giraffe return to their single forms. Microwave hum creeps back in; the congealing pasta sits like punishment.

*Why not me becomes why her; why Serafina first, why Serafina always, why Serafina forever sainted in death?*

Chrissy touches her flat belly, feels it hollow as a drum, hears the echo. *Infertile?* Maybe. Unchosen? Certainly.

Hope crackles, browns at the edges, curls. It burns to black ash so fast she tastes it on her tongue. The tarot deck snaps shut. The house exhales a long, cold draught as if someone has opened a door to winter.

She wipes the red lipstick away with the back of her hand, leaving a dirty rose smear across her palm like blood that won't clot, and goes back to the laptop. The cursor still blinks; steady, indifferent. One white square in a world of grey. Yes, the cursor still blinks; steady, very indifferent. One white square in a world of metallic grey on her unfinished novel; *Unreal in Love.*

***

**Author's Clinical Notes:**

This chapter is quiet on the surface.

But psychologically, it is seismic.

The date went well. There was chemistry. There was desire. There was mutual recognition.

And yet immediately afterwards, I turn inward and begin comparing myself to a dead woman. Not because she is present. Because she is feminine.

Or rather, because I imagine her to be.

Notice what happens.

I begin to divide women into categories:

*Soft.*

*Pink.*

*Velvet.*

*Rooted.*

Versus

*Steel.*

*Granite.*

*Fleet Street.*

*Hardened.*

This is not actually about her.

This is about my own split.

When a girl's body is invaded early, she often survives by armouring.

Competence becomes protection.

Intellect becomes shield.

Achievement becomes defence.

I went into journalism.

I faced violent men.

I interviewed killers.

I stood in courtrooms.

I called it bravery.

And it was.

But it was also a way of living in steel.

*Steel is powerful.*

*Steel is respected.*

*Steel does not blush.*

But steel does not ever soften.

And in this chapter, I realise something quietly devastating:

I do not feel feminine.

Not because I am not attractive.

Not because I am not sexual.

Because I am frozen.

Femininity, in the way I unconsciously defined it, meant receptivity.

*Warmth.*

*Softness.*

*Yielding without fear.*

But yielding in childhood with my adoptive family had once been dangerous.

So, I hardened.

And then I looked at other women; wives, mothers, pink softness and assumed they possessed something I had lost.

This is the tragedy.

We often mistake armour for identity.

I thought I was "just not that type of woman."

In truth, my softness was under lock.

And here is the cruel twist:

The more I felt frozen, the more I sought men of intensity.

Because intensity can thaw steel.

Or so I believed.

Facing serial killers.

Standing near violence.

Entering danger.

That was my unconscious attempt to reactivate heat.

If I can feel desire in the presence of danger, I am not numb.

But danger is not warmth.

It is voltage.

Voltage excites.

Warmth sustains.

I did not yet know the difference.

So, when I look at Seraphina in my imagination; sage green, velvet, quiet; I assume she possesses effortless femininity.

I rank myself beneath her.

This ranking is not about beauty.

It is about embodiment.

She feels like a woman.

I feel like a journalist pretending to be a woman.

That is the ache.

And this ache is shared by many women who have survived by competence.

You can be successful.

Articulate.

Strong.

Sexual.

And still feel internally exiled from softness.

The shopping scene matters.

Buying clothes.

Touching makeup.

Trying to feel younger.

This is not vanity.

It is rehearsal.

I am trying on embodiment again.

Trying to feel pink inside steel.

Trying to prove I have not missed the boat.

Marriage.

Motherhood.

Installation.

Underneath it all sits the question:

*Am I still viable?*

That question is brutal.

And rarely spoken aloud.

When a woman feels she has "hardened," she often fears she has forfeited tenderness.

But hardness is not loss of femininity.

It is adaptive survival.

Softness does not disappear.

It goes underground.

This chapter is where I begin to sense that I have been living in armour.

And armour is not the same as sovereignty.

Sovereignty is embodied calm.
Armour is defended intensity.
At this point in the story, I am still confusing the two.

# Chapter Eight. The Psychic.

*Poppy: To dream again. To forget again. The poppy was planted where no one would see it, blooming quietly in the aftermath of war.*

It had been a regular day when Nadine rang her.

"Hey Chris; you like spooky things; well, a girl in the hospital told me about this really talented, Psychic. I think you should go and see him; he'll actually tell you your future, or so she said! I couldn't wait to tell you. Hope it's to say good things about that Robert guy you've just been out with! He might be your Twin Flame! Quickly! Go find out!" she grinned.

The weather outside played its part, a drizzle. With the hope of stepping into the elusive realm of lunchtime camaraderie, with chit-chat with the others, she decided to venture to Mike's offices in Ballygowan.

She weaved through the lively, rain-kissed streets, feeling the pulse of the city. Vibrant shopfronts and the glow of streetlights create a kaleidoscope of colours as she approach Mike's place feeling shy and nervous all at the same time.

Mike's office is bathed in the soft glow of white candles. The rain outside taps on the windows. The room, adorned with mystical symbols, captivates her, and the eclectic scents create an atmosphere that transcends the usual mundane.

She shivers, and the air crackles, the scent of church incense weaves through the cosy space. In the dimly lit room with tangerine velvet cushions and scarlet chiffon curtains; Mike, a white-haired older gentleman with a kindly manner and intelligent grey blue eyes, welcomes her with a kind smile.

"Ah, you've been searching for something, haven't you, Chrissy?" Mike the Psychic's voice carries a resonance that draws her. "Let me reveal what the fates and my Spirit Guide have whispered to me about your journey. Yet you've your own Spiritual Guides, haven't you?"

"Yes, I have!"

Mike's eyes twinkled. "You've had experiences, haven't you? Unusual ones, perhaps involving spirit?"

"Yes."

Mike nodded, as if piecing together a puzzle.

'You're clairvoyant?

"Yes, I had a Spirit Guide called 'Keeper' and he comes and goes. But right now; I've not seen or heard from him."

"That can happen!"

"What about love, Mike? Will I ever know love? I haven't so far. I've recently met a man called Robert!"

"Ah, love," he continued. "A Twin Flame with the initial J. A sacred reunion of souls, halves of a cosmic whole is on the cards for you!"

The room seemed to hold its breath.

"J," she murmured, the letter resonating with newfound significance. "How will I meet this man who has the letter J in his name?"

Mike grinned. "It's something to do with a birthday! I don't know whose; but this J... he lives near or across the sea from where you were born!"

'J!"

"You're the only ones who can make each other happy; and once you meet; that's it for both of you; you won't ever be able to love another, even if you sell out your soul and marry someone else...! You are Twin Flames!"

She felt ecstatic. Though she also knew that she'd have to google the term, Twin Flames.

"Great, Chrissy, glad you're pleased. That'll be sixty-five pounds, please!"

She handed over the money, still absorbing the revelations and wondering if he wasn't a complete fake.

Soon as she stepped out into the drizzle, waves of doubt washed over her.

Wasn't this the same nonsense you hear in any fortune teller's booth?

She sighed, the bustling grey streets of Ballygowan a stark contrast to the ambiance of Mike's plush office.

The rain had subsided, leaving behind glistening streets and a fresh, invigorating scent. She decided to embrace the moment anyway.

.

A bustling café, tucked away in a corner of Ballygowan town, welcomes with the aroma of freshly brewed tea and the comforting warmth of the indoors.

Their hippy décor is eclectic yet cozy, with mismatched chairs and vintage teacups, creating a haven amidst the urban buzz.

She orders a pot of Earl Grey, its fragrant steam rising and mingling with the whispers of nearby conversations.

Rain-kissed windows offer a view of the lively street outside, where people with umbrellas stroll past, their reflections mingling with the city lights on the wet pavement.

As she sips the hot sweet tea, the intricate flavors swirl in her mouth, and the warmth spreads through her body. She orders a cake, bites into it and suddenly feels like Proust. The soft clinking of teaspoons against porcelain and the distant laughter of patrons mingles with the scent of cake, creating comfort.

The rain outside, the aroma of tea, and the gentle hum of conversation weave together, etching a memory of that lingers. In her mind's eye, she envisions the great loves of history; Napoleon and Josephine, whose passion and connection transcended time.

She mentally traverses the landscapes of legendary romances: the timeless allure of Romeo and Juliet, the enduring bond of Cleopatra and Mark Antony. Wondering will her own tale echo through the corridors of time, etching itself into the annals of great love stories.

She imagines J stepping into the narrative of her lonely life, their destinies converging like two stars in a grand ballet. Yet what of Robert? She so felt that he was some kind of missing part of her. Only Serafina stood in her way.

***

Her and Robert slipped into a dating rhythm after that first lunch, a soft, unspoken choreography of anticipation and discovery.

Robert would drive out to see her, a blue car humming steadily over familiar roads, and she would watch the countryside blur past in greens and greys, punctuated with tiny villages that smelled faintly of peat, rain, and frying oil from tiny takeaway shops.

The windows steamed with condensation, soft fog curling along the edges, and she pressed her forehead lightly to the glass, letting her mind wander to him, to the way he moved, the quiet confidence in the tilt of his head, the weight of his hand resting lightly on the gearstick.

Music played low from the stereo; a warm, slow jazz that seemed to match the rise and fall of her heartbeat and she let it fill the small space around them, drawing her into the rhythm of the journey.

One night, they walked hand in hand toward the cinema, lights flickering against wet pavements, the aroma of popcorn and coffee curling into the damp night air. Neon signs reflected in puddles like broken stained glass, and the occasional car swept past, tires hissing softly on the asphalt.

She laughed as he teased her about her seat choice, and she leaned into him, letting the closeness of their bodies hum between them.

Inside, the scent of buttered popcorn and chocolate mingled with the dim warmth of the theatre, the velvet seats pressing against her back, the low hum of anticipation in the dark.

The film played, but her attention drifted; to the press of his shoulder against hers, the faint warmth of his hand brushing her knee, the slow, deliberate rhythm of shared breaths.

Later, after the credits rolled, they wandered out into the night, wet pavement gleaming beneath streetlamps. The air smelled faintly of rain and warm stone, a smell that lingered on her clothes and hair, and she could feel the echo of the film mingling with her pulse.

He laughed softly at some private joke, and she felt a dizzy, spinning happiness. The streets seemed longer, more forgiving, the world smaller, contained, alive with possibility.

They paused at a corner, lights reflecting in puddles, and he brushed a stray curl from her face, thumb lingering, eyes catching hers in that slow, deliberate way that made her chest tighten and her mind blur.

***

Another mid-February afternoon was gilded in gold. They met for lunch at a pub just outside the town, a low ceiling, polished wood, the scent of roast and the faint tang of beer curling through the air.

Sunlight fell through small, paned windows, catching on the surface of the table, illuminating the faint motes of dust floating lazily. They shared plates of heavy, rich food; something roasted, fragrant, filling and she tasted the warmth and comfort in every bite.

Conversation meandered from trivial observations to confessions: the small humiliations of work, the eccentricities of friends, the oddities of the world. And yet, beneath it all, a current of tension ran between them, silent, invisible, something that made her pulse quicken even as she laughed.

She remembered the way he had brushed her hand lightly as he reached for a glass, the soft pressure that lingered a moment too long, the way the sunlight caught the edge of his dark hair and made it gleam golden in some places, almost like a halo.

She caught herself imagining Serafina in her place, imagining the ways the woman could haunt the small spaces between them, a spectre woven into the folds of memory and desire. The thought made her stomach tighten, a delicious shiver, and she sipped her wine, letting it warm her chest while her gaze lingered on him, on the rise and fall of his shoulders, on the curve of his jaw, on the depth in the blue eyes that had first caught at her heart.

The road wound through dense woodland, trees towering above them, their trunks slick with rain, leaves catching flecks of sunlight that managed to pierce the canopy. The air smelled of pine, damp earth, and wildflowers pressed close to the paths. Birds called across the glades, and somewhere a small brook babbled, its voice threading through the forest like a song she could not place.

His car slowed as they approached the lake, sunlight glinting off its surface, the water dark and reflective, catching every nuance of sky and tree, a mirror to their own restless, pulsing emotions.

She stepped out first, gravel crunching under her sandals, the sound strangely loud in the quiet of the glen. The wind lifted her hair, brushing it across her cheek, and she felt the warmth of the sun on her shoulders. He followed, coat collar turned up, eyes scanning the woods as if reading them, aware of every flicker of movement, every ripple of light.

They walked along the path skirting the lake, boots soft against the earth, the rhythm of their steps like a silent music, punctuated by laughter and quiet conversation.

At the water's edge, the world seemed to hold its breath. The lake shimmered, small ripples catching the sun, reeds swaying gently, birds skimming the surface with quiet urgency. She felt herself drawn to him, drawn by a pull she could neither name nor resist. His hand found hers, the touch deliberate, grounding, and yet igniting a fire beneath her skin.

The first lovemaking was a slow, delicious surrender.

Beside the lake, under the forgiving warmth of an unseasonably bright sun, they found a small patch of grass and laid a blanket, the earth cool beneath them, the scent of pine and wet leaves mingling with the heat of their skin.

Every touch, every brush of lips against lips, felt amplified, alive, a dialogue of sensation and awareness. She could feel the pulse of his heartbeat, the rhythm of breath against her ear, the tremor of desire that made her chest tight with both anticipation and delight.

The world narrowed to that small circle of warmth and sun, the shimmer of water, the rustle of leaves, the whisper of wind through branches. Music, imagined and internalised, threaded through her mind; a low, sensual jazz, the quiet pulse of strings, the soft swell of piano and she let it carry her, fold her into him, into the moment, until the edges of fear and doubt blurred, and only presence remained.

He ripped off her knickers and took her there and then up against a tree; so roughly it was almost like rape. As he pounded her so hard she felt as if she would split into two parts; she wondered were there someone observing them and then she realised that they were miles away in the wildness of the Gortin glen.

Later, lying against him on the blanket, she traced the line of his jaw with her fingertips, felt the warmth of his chest beneath her cheek, the way the sunlight caught the faint golden threads in his hair.

She closed her eyes and let the sounds, the smells, the heat of the sun, the pulse of his body, and the quiet lap of water against the shore fill her entirely. There was joy here, a fragile, vivid, electric joy, threaded with the shadow of anticipation, with the memory of risk, the whisper of danger pressing softly against her heart. It was cold and yet she felt so connected to nature; she felt as if she were something wild and free.

When they finally walked back through the woods, the paths damp beneath their feet, the forest alive with whispering leaves and distant birdcalls, she felt the world settle differently around her. Every glance, every brush of his hand, every shared smile carried a weight she had not expected, and yet she felt light, alive, as though the glen itself had witnessed, approved, and cradled the beginning of something fragile, thrilling, and wholly hers.

The drive back to Belfast was quieter than the outward journey, the blue car gliding over wet roads, tires whispering against asphalt slick with summer rain. Sunlight peeked through the clouds in pale streams, catching on the glint of his hair and the polished dash. She sat beside him, fingers brushing accidentally, deliberately, savouring the warmth and the hum of the car as the landscape rolled by. Music played low, a slow, jazzy melody that seemed to echo the rhythm of her pulse, each note threading through her chest, her thoughts, settling lightly like dust in the sun. She knew herself to be in love.

***

In the following days, life folded around their small rituals. He came to see her at odd hours, appearing at the door with a shy grin, a single flower sometimes, something bright against the dull grey of the Belfast streets.

They went to the cinema again, this time a quieter art-house theatre, seats soft, the smell of popcorn mixed with varnished wood. She laughed too loudly at an unexpected line in the film, and he nudged her gently, a shared joke that left her feeling dizzy, intoxicated with the simple pleasure of being with him.

Later, she discovered the thrill of ordinary errands layered with subtle tension. They went shopping, wandering along cobbled streets where small boutiques displayed handbags, scarves, delicate perfumes.

She lingered over soft leather, imagining it draped over her arm, while he examined the subtle gold clasp with a thoughtful frown. They tested lipsticks in tiny mirrors, the scent of vanilla and floral blends mingling with the faint dampness of the streets outside. A small, mischievous jealousy bubbled when he paused to ask about a bag she admired; her pulse quickened as she realised how much she wanted his attention, his focus, just for her.

He bought her a gold locket in a small old jewellers; an oval shape and delicate engraving up the edges. She knew that she would keep it forever and later clipped a lock of his silky dark hair and laid it inside of it as he tied it around her slim neck.

***

Conversations inevitably. turned, at first lightly, to Serafina. His voice was careful, measured, the occasional flicker of emotion behind the calm. She noticed it all: the way he paused, the light in his blue eyes dimming just for a heartbeat, the weight of his sigh as if carrying more than words could hold.

She pressed herself to listen, to understand, to trace the invisible threads of his past that wove quietly, insistently, between them. And yet she felt a pull, a dizzying attraction that made her pulse flare, legs weak, and stomach curl with anticipation and fear.

One afternoon, he suggested a drive back into the Glen again where they had first made love, this time a shorter, sun-warmed walk along the lake's edge.

The air smelled of pine, wet earth, and wildflowers pressed close to the paths. The sun glinted off the water, sending sparks across her eyes, and she felt herself dissolve into the sensation: warmth, wind, the brush of his hand grazing hers, the weight of his body beside her.

Words became secondary to presence; laughter faded into silence, into the hum of the world, until she felt him close enough that the warmth between them had a gravity, pulling her toward him, toward something urgent and fragile.

They paused at a small jetty, the lake dark and still beneath their feet. She felt the brush of his fingers against her wrist, the soft press of his lips at her temple, the teasing weight of his gaze. And in that quiet, golden hour, desire took her fully, unspoken and unrelenting. Their first lovemaking in the Glen had been tender; this, now, was deeper.

He made her bend over a rock and took her from behind urging her to call out in pleasure and she imagined that she could feel eyes on her; peering out of the dark wood as he pulled her around shoving his manhood into her open mouth and then whipping her buttocks with a branch that had fallen from a tree. She felt alive, raw, and dizzy with erotic sensation, the world narrowing to the small space they occupied, the sun catching flecks of gold in his hair, the lake murmuring beside them as they climaxed in unison.

When they returned to the car, sun-warmed and flushed, she noticed a subtle change in herself.

The sharpness, the metallic edge she carried, softened slightly in his presence, but not entirely; just enough that the world felt more immediate, more urgent.

She found herself noticing small things: the way he adjusted his sleeve, the quiet intensity in his blue eyes, the moments of hesitation before a smile.

She realised that every sexual encounter carried layers; laughter, warmth, intimacy; but also shadow, small hints of darkness that pricked at the edges.

Back at home, she worked at her desk, coffee steaming beside her, while snippets of his presence lingered in the room. She caught herself thinking about him in corners of her mind she could not entirely control: the curve of his hand, the way his voice caught on certain words, the small gestures that were now ineffably his. Yet alongside this warmth, a whisper of unease persisted. She remembered news reports from years ago: a serial killer loose in Tyrone, long blonde hair, meticulous, careful, untraceable.

And though part of her knew it was absurd, a private, irrational thread of fear began to wind through her thoughts, tugging at the edges of trust, teasing the shadow of possibility that something in him was darker than the bright, warm man she had come to crave. The confession so his sexual fantasies were all about tying her up; whipping her buttocks. They always had to have sex outside where she feared that others had eyes all over them as they fucked.

***

She told Nadine about her fears one evening over coffee, the sun slanting through the window, casting bars of light across the table.

"Just because he's a bit of a kinky sod, doesn't make him a serial killer; you've spent too long studying those creeps!"

'Yeah, you're right; I'm being nuts!"

Words spilled freely, laughter punctuating caution, a subtle note of envy lingering beneath every smile.

They talked of charm, of quiet weight, of the unspoken pull of attraction, and yet of the small hints of menace, the questions left unanswered. Nadine tilted her head, eyes sharp, amused but probing, and she felt herself both grateful and nervous, as if every word carried consequences she could not foresee.

Later, Pauline joined them, coffee cups clinking in a small, busy café, and the three of them wandered to shops, lingering over handbags and scarves, testing perfume, brushing fingers over satin and silk. Teasing filled the air, but underneath it, a faint, sharp tension threaded through; a tiny, prickling jealousy, a whisper of fear, and a subtle, intoxicating thrill.

Chrissie realised how fragile the balance was between desire and anxiety, between comfort and dread, between what was present and what might yet emerge from shadows.

By the end of the day, walking back through streets damp with rain and glinting with the reflections of streetlamps, she felt herself suspended between two worlds: the joy of intimacy and discovery, the warmth of touch and laughter, and the quiet, insistent suggestion that she was seeing only what he allowed her to see.

Chrissie felt the tension coil, a pulse beneath the skin, a whispering awareness that the man she desired so fiercely could, in some quiet, unimaginable way, also be the source of a brooding danger.

**Author's Clinical Notes:**

This chapter is not about clairvoyance.

It is about certainty.

When you grow up without stability, you crave inevitability.

A psychic offers inevitability.

"He is the one."

"You are twin flames."

"He lives across the sea from where you were born."

"He is the only one who can make you happy."

Those sentences land like oxygen to someone who has lived in ambiguity.

Ambiguity is intolerable when attachment has been unstable.

So, prophecy feels soothing.

Twin flames.

Soulmates.

*Destined union.*

These concepts are intoxicating because they remove choice.

If he is fated, I do not have to evaluate.

If he is written, I do not have to risk.

If we are twin flames, the volatility is sacred, not alarming.

This is where myth replaces discernment.

I did not just fall in love with Robert.

I folded him into a cosmology.

He became J.

He became the man from across the sea.

He became destiny correcting my childhood fracture.

And here is the dangerous part:

If someone is fated to heal you, you do not need to heal yourself.

You wait for ignition.

You wait for the golden egg to explode.

You wait for sex beside a stream to become transformation.

This is not stupidity.

*It is spiritualised longing.*

Twin flame ideology is particularly seductive to women who have experienced emotional instability. It reframes volatility as depth. It reframes obsession as divine mirroring. It reframes suffering as purification.

*"Your soulmate will trigger you."*

*"Your twin flame will expose your wounds."*

These statements can be true in healthy relationships.

But they can also romanticise dysregulation.

*I believed that great love would thaw me.*

That the right man; intense, slightly dangerous, mythic; would awaken my femininity and dissolve my steel.

So, I did what I had always done.

I layered.

Robert was not just a widower.

He became prophecy.

He was not just a man from Tyrone.

He became the man across the sea.

He was not just attractive.

He became archetype.

And when we lay beside the stream; beautiful, cinematic, elemental; I believed something had begun that would cure me.

I did not yet understand that erotic sovereignty does not arrive through another person's presence.

It arrives through inhabiting yourself fully.

The psychic chapter matters because it reveals the mechanism:

When we cannot trust ourselves, we outsource authority.

To psychics.

To fate.

To mythology.

To men.

And when the relationship later destabilises; as relationships do; the fall feels cosmic.

Not relational.

Because you did not lose a man.

You lost destiny.

That is a much deeper collapse.

This chapter is not romantic.

It is revealing.

It shows the moment where longing turned into belief.

And belief is harder to disentangle than attraction.

I'd mixed it all up in a melange and thrown it at Robert. He's now responsible for me coming back to life.

I didn't want a boyfriend.

I wanted resurrection.

# Chapter Nine: Gortin Glen, Tyrone.

Camellia (Pale Pink)

*The camellia holds its silence. In Japan, they were once left on graves; not as symbols of love, but as apologies for what could not be spoken.*

It was a wet Thursday and she was in Tyrone. They'd decided to hike in Gorton Glen; the same place Robert had played as a child and they had first made love.

They tramped for miles, the weak sun filtering through dripping tree tops. The mountains loomed, the air filled with the scent of green moss and purple lichen. In the deep woodlands, fear of being lost crept in. Yet she watched him and felt safe beside him.

The weather had started out rainy, then sunny; but it was an unseasonably wet, hot April afternoon. Robert stood and watched her as rain hit their faces, and they stopped in a clearing.

Golden sun-light mingled with the rain, creating an eerie other worldly atmosphere. The woods enveloped them both in uncertainty and the haunting presence of his grief of his wife made her feel as if she was carrying a weight, or an ache. She so wanted him as her very own. She had begun to hate Serafina.

The fine mist of rain draped a cold veil over the mystical Irish landscape. The chill crept into their bones as the wild bluebells carpeted the dark woods, exuding a heavenly fragrance.

Distant train horns echoed through remote Irish stations, punctuating the eerie silence.

"I feel as if I'm falling in love with you: do you feel the same way about me?" he asked.

"Maybe," she replied, fearing that if she admitted that she was feeling exactly the same he would lose interest in her.

He found a circle of trees. He took her to its dark heart.

"Lay down, here on this soft bed of moss, Chrissy, I want to show you exactly how I feel about you whilst we're hidden by this glorious nature."

Sea-green ivy vines snaked along the icy ground, and wild flowers painted the surroundings in hues of pink and marmalade yellow. His skin felt cold and smooth as he undressed. Moans echoed through the forest as he pressed into her bones, the weight of history between them.

The trees leaned and swayed, like curious onlookers, as rainwater sparkled like crushed diamonds over the overgrown grass beneath their naked lovemaking deep within the Gortin Glen.

They lay naked like two babes in the wood.

A hailstorm unleashed its fury, turning the forest bed into a merciless arena. They stood up and went to the edge of the circle of trees. They watched the chunks of white hail. The hail battened the glen as if in fury. They shivered naked.

As the storm gradually subsided, a bright rainbow appeared over the circle of trees. A spider's web glistened in the dew, a delicate masterpiece against the backdrop of nature.

She gasped at the abundance of the natural world.

"Are you my Twin Flame?"

'I don't know Chrissy, I don't even know what that means,' he said softly. "Do you regret this?"

"No, Robert," she replied back. "Yet sometimes I don't know where we're going."

"Give me time; you know I've just come out of a marriage. Once bitten twice shy."

It felt like a rejection but it felt as if the Gods were speaking to them through the sky.

Hours later, in his Tyrone house, she sat across from him sharing a meal of his favourite, Beef Bourguignonne and oaky white wine. His eyes held a cat-and-mouse intensity as he revealed his loneliness after Seraphina passed and left him.

Alone in his bathroom, wearing a lilac cord skirt and floral blouse she pondered the wedding photo of he and his dead wife on one of the wooden shelves holding cosmetics that had to be hers; a flat bottle of White Linen perfume.

She prepared for the night ahead, spraying on the white floral perfume and fixing her clothes and lilac lace bra.

His forceful knock interrupted her thoughts. They ventured to the veranda, sharing Budweiser under a starlit sky. The breeze carried the scent of the river, and memories of their forest encounter lingered. Robert's sexy smile hinted at something more physical as the night unfolded in a silent, eerie wait.

In the half-light, his penetrating gaze and coy smile set the stage for what lay ahead.

The heat in the house wrapped around her, mingling with nerves and hunger after a hearty meal of steak and roast potatoes cooked expertly by him, a dish-clothe flung over his arm like a professional chef. The weighty red wine flowed freely as they both sat before the crackling fire, casting a rosy glow on her relaxed face.

"So! You and I! You came like a ray of sunshine into a dark room, Chrissy. I was lost." She nodded, as he stood up his face looking oddly excited. "You must be tired though now. Let me show you to the spare room."

Grateful for his good manners, she welcomed the respite from continuous company and time to be alone to review their fast-moving love story.

He stood up, declaring, "I won't go near your bedroom. Let you have your space." His laughter filled the room, but then a serious expression crossed his face. "I've not had feelings as strong as this about anyone in a while." He closed the distance, scrutinising her as if resentful for wanting her so intensely.

"Oh," she stammered.

"What about you?" His enigmatic demeanor unsettled her, yet an odd familiarity lingered.

"I don't know. No idea how I feel," she lied, wanting to stay in control; yet driven mad with love for him.

Composing himself, his devouring eyes hinted at a physical hunger behind a thin veneer of politeness.

Retreating to the bedroom, she stared at her reflection.

Feigning activity in the bathroom, she listened to his proposition of sitting on the veranda overlooking a river, a secret haven for a night-cap.

Stars adorned the ceiling like silver foil as he anticipated her thoughts, presenting her with another ice-cold Budweiser.

Swigging the drink, a warmth enveloped her. Relaxed in her demure flowery blouse and a modest green skirt, she savoured the scent of his pale skin and his distinct aftershave.

Insects hummed in the warm air as they stood by the river, memories of their love-making lingering. Intent on unraveling his mystery, she sipped beer, contemplating a poem.

*Here I sit in the cold stone dread. The ash in the fireplace, the cold ice of my heart. This is an empty House; this House is a House of Mourning...*

Robert's penetrating stare shifted to a smile, almost coy. He reached for her hand, but she pulled away, glancing around, unsure of what awaited. A shroud of white mist descended swiftly, ensnaring the garden in an eerie embrace.

“Serafina has gone, Chrissy, please get over her. It’s just you and I Chrissy, that’s the reality. But do you want to open your heart to love? Because I don’t do casual.”

She felt suddenly breathless. "Nor do I Robert but I can’t. I can’t. I don’t let ever people come near me," she protested, rising and heading toward the river, an internal urge compelling her to walk endlessly into its cold depths.

"The river's got a very slippery bank. You'll fall," he warned as the mist thickened, rain descending, and the garden plunged into darkness.

"Can't. I can't. I can't," reverberating as the wind flapped the tarpaulin on a moored boat. Her reflection in the boat's window shocked her with its aging. "I'm in my thirties, still hoping to marry and have a child," she yelled

Robert materialised behind her.

"I want this love to grow and who knows where it'll take us. If we had a child between us, what would you call it?"

She felt like crying; there was no child and that was the truth of her messy little nonsense life.

"Cloud."

Robert, intense and impassioned, declared, "I'll give you what you want! I'll give you, Cloud! I'll give you release, an orgasm. A marriage, with a man who gets you...sees you."

Surprised at his speech, she replied, "Robert don't lie to me."

The rain intensified as he seized her, ripping her clothes off and following by tearing at his own; their naked forms dancing like a mad ballerina in the wet mud, screams echoing in the garden. "Say it!" he urged.

"This is good," she mumbled in inexperienced delight. "I want you, Robert," she admitted, prompting a grin from him.

"You fell in love with me at first sight, didn't you? I saw you. I saw you being turned on by me. Then you couldn't stop yourself." His eyes locked onto hers. "You want my cock," he emphasised, pressing her against the garden wall, laughing deeper.

Amidst the dark water's murmur, Robert led her back into the warm house, running a bath surrounded by scented candles. The intimacy continued as he dried her with a warm blue towel. In the kitchen, a homemade soup awaited he had made with ready chopped vegetables, bringing warmth to the cold night.

As they sat in the cosy kitchen, the conversation turned to her career. "It's so specialised," she remarked, broaching the topic of a recent client who had depression and anxiety.

Later, Robert dressed her in his pajamas with unusual tenderness. In the spare room, thoughts churned. Unable to sleep, she ventured downstairs in the chilly night, discovering a hidden storeroom with a computer. She turned it on and there it was hundreds of photographs of both of them enjoying married life with two children. She wished she hadn't looked.

Suddenly she was there beside her.

'He's my husband and he's not as fucking la la lovely as this all seems. My husband murdered me. He put it in my lunch ... Mr. Master Chef. It was invisible poison he bought online that left no trace. I just keeled over at work."

Chrissy turned to face the ghost; "You're a liar; you're a fucking greasy liar jealous of me for being alive and having his warm cock inside of me."

Seraphina grinned maliciously. "Wait until he gets sick of you. Don't be seeing Robert as the answer to your prayers. Robert isn't the answer to any woman's prayers. Robert's every woman's worse nightmare. "

***

The morning sun shone cruelly through the window. Chrissy blinked, opened her eyes, and remembered where she was.

She opened the window and craned her neck out at the Irish countryside. It smelled like a holiday haven. The freshness of the air was intoxicating. Downstairs, she could smell eggs and bacon cooking and hear the sizzling from the greasy hob.

There was a strong scent of fruity pineapple soap and mint toothpaste in the bathroom. On the shelves were deodorants, musky aftershaves, and some pills in amber-coloured bottles. In the main bedroom, behind a closed door, she found his marital bed with pale primrose-yellow sheets. It was still impregnated with the warmth of his body, and his sweat had dampened the yellow cotton.

She went downstairs, and he appeared, bringing out a hot cooked breakfast. Soft fried eggs, toast, and baked beans. Strongly brewed hot tea in thick green mugs. They sat silently, chewing their sausage and bacon at the table.

Later, after breakfast, they drove along low country roads. Robert often slowed down the car to lean over and kiss her.

It was another perfectly motionless day of early summer, hazy and honey-coloured, with towering pine trees meeting the aqua blue of a silent sky. He looked at her seriously as he held her hand, rubbing it with his thumb in the heavy sunlight coming through the open window of the car.

"There's a lot of this in our relationship, isn't there?"

"Touching? Yes. Is that bad?"

"No, no ....just noticing!"

He pulled the car over and went into a garage shop to buy them both choc-ices. Chrissy opened her door and followed him into the old-fashioned shop next to the garage, with its sacks of potatoes outside and postcards of the local Irish villages in wire stands.

She marvelled at the strange things they had for sale; old-fashioned sweets in huge glass jars and dusty children's books.

"Here's a Magnum; like 'em?"

"Thanks."

The shopkeeper stared at them both an odd look on her face.

'Ohh err.... love is!!"

Chrissy felt a warmth flood her. The world was confirming it. It was *real.* She stared out of the window as she nibbled at the delicious choc-ice.

The countryside passing outside the car window was reminiscent of Tuscany; old homes and poppy fields. Robert had fallen silent. The late summer day unfolded, hazy and honey-colored, with vast pine trees meeting the silent aqua blue sky.

An hour later, they pulled into a thin country lane. An archway of trees led down to a large empty house at the end of a twisting driveway. She blinked as they drove slowly down the private drive lined with cup-like yellow flowers and large weeping willows.

"This place is so intriguingly beautiful from the outside." The magnificent house loomed large in front of them; a handsome structure built of stone; the grounds were alighted with purple forget-me-nots.

"This is where I always went as a child," said Robert dreamily. "Now, I'm thinking of buying it to start again. Like it? Just you, me; my two children. Then a child of our own! What say you?"

She couldn't speak she felt so moved.

Two iron lions guarded the entrance, a front door covered in dust with a faded brass door knocker. Through the letterbox, she could see the wallpaper and imagined how its inhabitants had once lived. She didn't know how to react – what to say. Here it was; it was happening to her what happened to all other women, or so it seemed; meeting a partner; falling in love; making beautiful dreamy plans. She'd feared that she was to be overlooked. *Left out.*

"I-I-I'd love to live here," was all she could manage.

Back in the car, she gazed out of the window. She could see herself in the wing mirror. Her make-up was smudged, and it was a hot day. The sun made her eyes ache, and she thought she looked old. An old princess, still hoping to marry.

*I used to dream of a prince who would kiss me, waking me from my prison of ice. Now he has come and wants to bring me to a kingdom, that beautiful house where we'll live in happiness with his children, Kira and Jon, and our own baby on the way ... I must mother them ...guide them ...make sure that they have good lives!*

Chrissy put on some mascara from her make-up bag and blinked in the wing mirror. She hadn't spent much time with his children bar the odd family dinner and she both liked and wanted them to accept her; but she knew it was far too early and they were teenagers who had their own lives.

"Are you OK, Robert? You look so white."

He replied without meeting her eyes. "Yeah, fine."

Long, low stone walls curved over the thin country roads. The car went over bumps and holes. She took off her cardigan and stared out of the window, enjoying the sight of cows, sheep, and horses in the passing fields.

He drove on in silence, then said, "Do you believe, Chris, that we all have different sides?"

"How do you mean?"

"Relax, Chris, you're awfully tense."

Ten minutes later, they came to a lake. As they walked down to the wood, they passed a magnificent waterfall. Past the gushing falls set in the side of a mountain, there was a lover's seat.

Robert sat down and smiled.

"The waterfall looks gold to me. Does it to you?" He looked at her carefully, as if it mattered how she replied. The cold, frothing waterfall thundered in front of them as they sat beneath it on the lover's bench, listening to the splash as the water hit the bottom. It was deafening.

"It's the sun shining on it." She could barely hear her own voice, drowned out as it was by the waterfall.

Robert took a deep breath. "They say only those in love see the water as gold! Chrissy, I truly love you."

She gazed up at the blue summer sky.

"Robert, you're mad! And yes, the water, ha, ....its shining gold."

**Author's Clinical Notes:**

I need to say something that may not be fashionable.

I was not wrong to want myth.

I was not naïve.

I was not immature.

I was not "avoidant of real love."

I wanted voltage.

I wanted weather.

I wanted land and sky and sex that felt like it cracked something open.

I wanted to be met in a way that rearranged me.

And I do not apologise for that.

On the wet Thursday in April 2003; when I lay naked in that circle of trees and the hail came down and then the sun broke through and there was a rainbow, I did not feel delusional. I felt finally alive.

I felt chosen.

I felt as though something in the universe had finally acknowledged me.

I didn't just make love in Gortin Glen; it was a ritual.

*Circle of Trees.*

*Hail.*

*Thunder.*

*Sun breaking through.*

*Rainbow.*

People like to mock this kind of love.

They prefer the language of fish fingers and toilet roll. They prefer the practical, the manageable, the socially approved. They say that's what lasts. They say that's maturity.

But here is what I have always believed:

*Most people never touch myth.*

They start with compatibility and stay there.

They build something decent and stable and call it depth.

*They never enter the forest.*

And because they never enter the forest, they tell themselves the forest doesn't exist. They never hit the forest-hail-rainbow voltage. And they quietly resent the myth that they never had. They defend ordinariness because it prevents them from longing.

I did not want a man to share a shopping list with.

I wanted to feel as if I had stepped into something older than language.

And I did.

That is not nothing.

But here is the part I did not understand at the time.

I had split love into two camps:

1. *Mythic, electric, consuming, destined.*
2. *Dead, banal, endured.*

There was no middle ground in my nervous system.

If it wasn't myth, it was mediocrity.

If it wasn't voltage, it was suffocation.

I thought ordinariness was death.

And perhaps for me, at that time, it was.

Because ordinariness felt like invisibility.

*Like being settled for.*

*Like being tolerated.*

*Like being endured.*

I did not want to be endured.

**I wanted to be burned for.**

What I didn't see was this: myth cannot stay at fever temperature forever.

Fever is not false; it's just unsustainable.

Bodies cannot live at that pitch.

No human being can permanently occupy destiny. They get tired. They forget things. They get distracted. They become human.

And when the human entered, I experienced it as betrayal.

Not disappointment.

Betrayal.

When the height softened, I felt abandoned.

That was my fracture.

Healthy couples do not live in myth permanently. They visit it. They survive the descent from voltage into continuity.

I had never learned how to descend.

Because in my childhood, calm was not safety.

Calm was the pause before something invasive.

*Storm felt familiar.*

*Storm felt honest.*

So, when love became steady instead of mythic, I interpreted steadiness as loss.

I did not want fish fingers and toilet roll because, to me, that symbolised diminishment.

*Containment.*

*Shrinking.*

I had spent my childhood being invaded. I would not then spend my adulthood being domesticated.

That refusal was not arrogance.

It was sovereignty trying to form.

But here is the nuance I am only beginning to grasp:

I was not actually addicted to chaos. I was addicted to aliveness. And I had only ever felt aliveness at high intensity. I had never experienced aliveness inside grounded love.

So, I assumed it didn't exist.

In that glen, in that circle of trees, I wasn't just making love to a man.

I was trying to secure permanence through symbolism.

*If the weather responded, it must be real.*

*If the sky split open, it must be ordained.*

*If there was a rainbow, it must be safe.*

I was trying to stabilise love through myth because I did not trust stability on its own.

And underneath all of it was a single question:

Can I inhabit desire without being consumed?

That question has followed me through serial killers, through widowers, through fantasies of destiny, through twin flame ideology.

It was never about drama.

It was about sovereignty.

If I could stand naked in myth and not disappear, I would finally be real.

What I did not yet understand is that sovereignty is not proven in storm.

It is proven in continuity. It is proven when voltage does not require catastrophe. It is proven when a woman can feel alive on a wet Tuesday afternoon without needing the sky to split open.

I do not regret the myth.

I needed it.

But I am beginning to see that the problem was not that ordinary love exists. The problem was that I believed ordinary love meant diminishment. I could not yet imagine a love that held voltage and continuity in the same body.

And so, when myth softened into humanity, I experienced humanity as failure.

This chapter is the high point.

It is also the blueprint of my blind spot.

*I wanted transcendence without descent.*

*I wanted fire without ash.*

*I wanted destiny without dishes.*

And that equation does not exist.

Not because love is small.

But because human bodies are finite.

**The forest was real.**

**The storm was real.**

**My desire was real.**

But I was trying to solve a lifetime wound with a single mythic union.

That is too much weight for any man to carry.

And it was too much weight for me to sustain.

The fever was not wrong.

But it was not the whole story.

# Chapter Ten – Press Cuttings.

*Jasmine: fragrant only at night. It speaks of love that awakens after dark; sweet and intoxicating, and gone by morning.*

She began to notice it the way you notice a song before you realise it has been following you all day. At first it was nothing. A television left on while she boiled the kettle. The low mutter of a presenter. Archive footage. A grainy still. The word Derry sliding past without snagging.

She barely looked up.

Later it happened again.

She was sitting at the small table by the window with her notebook open, pen resting against the page, the city dim and rain smeared beyond the glass.

She'd been trying to write. Something ordinary. Something safe. A paragraph that would not reach too far into the dark. The television murmured in the background, the way she liked it when she was alone, sound as a companion rather than a demand.

Then she heard it. A phrase. A date. Old footage again. The murders in Derry.

She froze with the pen still touching the page.

Long blonde hair, the reporter said. A teenager at the time. No arrests ever made. It was the serial killings again, they never seemed to be off the news.

She felt something cold and electric pass through her chest.

She turned the volume up.

It made no sense. It should not have meant anything. It was history. It was old. It was the kind of thing that came around every few years on late night television, repackaged as mystery, as nostalgia for fear.

And yet she could not shake the way her body reacted whenever she heard about the Derry Murders, the sudden awareness of her own breathing, the way her skin tightened along her arms.

She thought of him saying it lightly, almost carelessly. 'I used to have long blonde hair. I was not always dark.' The way he had smiled when he said it, as if offering her something intimate, something unguarded.

She had laughed then. She had touched his arm. She had thought it was charming.

Now the memory rearranged itself.

She told herself she was being ridiculous. This was what she did. This was her old habit, her old curse of investigating and meeting serial killers.

She hunted for danger when things felt too good. She had always done that. She had dated men she did not really want because they were manageable. Because she could see their flaws clearly and feel superior to them.

She had tried to hammer them into a shape they would never fit, mistaking effort for intimacy. And when something arrived that felt effortless, when desire came without struggle, when affection felt natural rather than negotiated, she mistrusted it.

A gift horse, she thought. Always looking into its mouth.

Still, she could not stop obsessing over the Derry Murders from decades ago carried out by a teenager with long flowing blonde hair.

***

Over the following weeks it kept happening. A documentary here. A radio discussion there. A newspaper headline glimpsed on a free sheet left on the train. She would tell herself it was coincidence. That she was simply noticing it now because her mind had been primed by the Derry Murders in True Crime podcasts on You Tube.

But the repetition of fear wore her down. Each mention pressed deeper, like water wearing a channel through stone.

She began to feel watched by the serial murder story itself.

At night she dreamed of roads and trees and the colour grey. She dreamed of being followed without ever seeing who followed her. She woke with her heart racing, the echo of a voice she could not quite place lingering in the room.

Serafina came then, not all at once, not fully formed.

At first it was only a feeling, a pressure in the air, a sense of being crowded even when she was alone. A chill that did not come from the window. A thought that did not feel like her own.

You are asking the wrong questions, the thought said.

She tried to ignore it. She made lists. She cleaned the kitchen. She went for long walks to tire herself out.

She told herself she was spiralling because she was happy, because happiness destabilised her more than misery ever had.

But the forensic investigator in her woke up anyway.

One afternoon she found herself standing outside the newspaper library, the old habit returning with muscle memory ease. The smell of paper and dust hit her as soon as she went in. It felt like coming home to a former life.

She signed her name without thinking. She asked for the archives without explanation.

She told herself she was only curious.

She sat at a long wooden table with the files spread out in front of her. Dates. Names. Black and white photographs. Headlines that had once screamed and now whispered.

The victims blurred into one another, young faces frozen mid smile, lives reduced to paragraphs and speculation. The descriptions repeated. The hair. The age.

The years stretching back further than she expected, back to a time when he would have been young, impressionable, unformed.

She did the maths without wanting to.

She felt sick.

There were gaps. Of course there were gaps. No clear suspect. No resolution. A case that had cooled and then frozen entirely. But there were details that snagged her attention.

A location that matched something he had once mentioned casually. Broken matches left beside the bodies and she had seen him pick up a toothpick in a restaurant and break it in just that same way.

A phrase used by a witness that echoed something he had said in a different context. Each connection was flimsy on its own. Together they formed a web that tightened around her chest.

She pushed the files away and pressed her palms flat against the table.

This is how psychotic paranoia begins, she thought.

That night she didn't turn her television on. The silence felt heavier than noise. She sat on the bed with her notebook and tried to write her novel, but every sentence collapsed into the same thoughts.

If this was true, if even a fraction of it was true, then everything she felt had been built on a lie. Her attraction. Her tenderness. Her trust. All of it contaminated.

And yet another voice rose to counter it. A quieter one. A voice that sounded like love.

*You know him.*

But did she.

Serafina appeared fully then, not as a ghost with edges and form, but as presence. As certainty. As something that slid into her thoughts with terrible intimacy.

'He did it,' Serafina said. 'He did it then and he did it to me.'

She covered her ears as if that could help stop the voices.

'He was young,' Serafina continued.

Her stomach clenched.

"And you," Serafina said softly, "...you've often made him feel small."

She slid down the wall and sat on the floor, her back pressed hard against it as if she could anchor herself to something solid.

"This is not real," she whispered.

But Serafina only smiled, or what felt like a smile.

"You wanted the truth," she said. "This *is* the truth; your lover's dangerous."

Images flooded her. His hands on the steering wheel. The woodland road. The way he watched her sometimes when he thought she was not looking. The number plate that had made her laugh and then unsettled her.

The sudden flares of jealousy that had flickered and died without explanation. All of it rearranged itself into something darker, something more coherent and therefore more terrifying.

She thought of how good it had felt. How rare that had been for her. How she had finally believed she might be safe inside love rather than merely adjacent to it.

She understood then how fear worked. Not as a scream but as a whisper that pretended to be reason. It did not say run. It said investigate. It said protect yourself. It said this is what intelligent women do.

By morning she was exhausted.

She looked at herself in the mirror and barely recognised the woman staring back. Her eyes were too bright. Her face too pale. She had not slept and it showed with the grey splodges and bags under her eyes. She knew, with a clarity that frightened her, that she could not go on like this; it was ruining her health.

That whether the danger was real or imagined, something had already broken. The innocence of her feeling. The ease of her trust. She had crossed a threshold she could not uncross.

***

She met Nadine and Pauline the following morning, as planned, though nothing inside her had shifted.

The Lisburn Road café was already loud when she arrived, steam rising from the espresso machine, cutlery clinking, the smell of frying fat and toast thick in the air.

It was one of those places that pretended to be effortless and bohemian while actually running on military precision and caffeine.

They were already there. Nadine in sunglasses she did not need indoors, hair pulled back tight, scrolling on her phone. Pauline opposite her, cardigan shrugged off one shoulder, attacking a plate of food with unapologetic pleasure.

"You look knackered," Pauline said without looking up. "Sit down before you fall down."

Nadine glanced up and frowned. "Actually yes. You look pale and haggard. Are you eating again, or are you on one of your spiritual fasts."

She slid into the chair and wrapped her hands around the mug Nadine pushed toward her. The heat grounded her slightly.

"I am eating," she said. "I had soup."

"Soup isn't food," Nadine said. "Soup is water with ideas."

Pauline spoke, mouth full of sausage. "Let her speak; this guy is ruining her damn life."

She hesitated. The moment stretched. Around them plates were arriving. Eggs glistened. Bacon curled. Someone laughed too loudly at a nearby table.

"It *is* Robert," she said finally. "I think he might have murdered his wife."

Both women froze.

Then Nadine burst out laughing.

"O' for fuck's sake."

Pauline wiped her mouth carefully and leaned back.

"Here we go with the forensic psychotherapy."

"I'm deadly serious," she said softly. 'I also believe that Robert is the man responsible for the Derry murders, years ago as a teenager."

Nadine shook her head, smiling. "I've seen a movie about that on Netflix. Chrissy, you do one nice normal thing and immediately turn it into an unsolved crime."

"This isn't funny," she whispered, and hated how defensive she sounded.

Pauline studied her more closely now. "All right," she said. "Say it again. Slowly."

She took a breath.

"As you know already; he's a widower. His wife died young. The circumstances are vague. And there were these murders years ago. Where he grew up near Derry and well ... he fits the description."

Silence fell between them, thinner this time.

Nadine lifted an eyebrow. "Fits the description of what. A man."

"Long blonde hair," she said. "When he was younger. He told me that himself."

Pauline snorted. "Chrissie! Half the men in the country had long blonde hair around that era. it was in fashion. At one point; it was practically compulsory."

"I keep seeing it on television," she offered, ignoring Pauline. "Documentaries. Articles. It's everywhere."

Nadine leaned forward. "This is Ireland; it's our news! Chrissie it's you who's everywhere," she said gently. "You're primed. You've an ex-private investigator's brain and a psychotherapist's heart. It is a lethal combination. Life isn't a drama; it's really all quite boring."

Pauline reached across and stole Nadine's hash brown.

"You're catastrophising. Women do this when they actually care about a new man."

She bristled. "Well, I don't."

"I'll bet you do! Pauline offered. "You've dated men you barely tolerated for years. Men who bored you senseless. And now someone turns up who actually lights you up and suddenly he's Jack the Ripper."

Nadine nodded; her mouth full of toast.

"You like puzzles more than happiness. Happiness scares you. You think if it arrives without pain attached it must be a trick."

Chrissie stared down at her untouched food. The eggs had gone cold.

"But you guys; what if I'm right, she said quietly. What if my body knows something my mind's trying to ignore. That he's a vicious lady-killer."

Nadine snorted and Pauline softened. She always did first.

"Love," she began gently. "Your body also once thought a man who could not say your name properly was the love of your life. Your instincts are brilliant but they're not infallible."

Nadine reached for her hand. "You've not said anything about him actually being violent. Or cruel. Or strange in real ways."

"He gets jealous," she said. "Sometimes. Small things."

"Men often get jealous," Nadine said. "Women get jealous. It doesn't make them murderers."

"And his dead wife," Pauline added. "She died young and unexpected; but that doesn't make him guilty. It makes him tragic."

Chrissie felt suddenly foolish. Exposed. Like a child who'd taken a nightmare into daylight only to see it shrink.

"I just have this feeling, she said. Like something watching me."

Pauline smiled kindly. "That's called falling in love."

Nadine raised her coffee. "To women who overthink everything and still survive."

They clinked mugs. The noise of the café rushed back in around them. Someone spilled sugar. Someone laughed again.

She smiled, because that was what one did among friends. She ate a forkful of eggs. They tasted of nothing.

As they stood to leave, Nadine squeezed her shoulder.

"Don't ruin this for yourself before it's even begun," she warned. "You deserve something good without turning it into a crime scene."

Outside, the air was sharp and cold. The city moved as it always did, indifferent to her private dread.

She walked away from them feeling both reassured and strangely alone. Their laughter echoed in her ears, but beneath it something else stirred. A quieter voice. Patient. Waiting. Serafina did not need to argue with her friends.

She only needed time.

***

**Author's Clinical Notes:**

Jasmine; fragrant only at night. It speaks of love that awakens after dark, sweet and intoxicating, and gone by morning.

I began to notice it the way you notice a song before you realise it has been following you all day.

The suspicion.

At first it was nothing.

Just a thought passing through.

He had long blonde hair once. The Derry murders had involved someone with long blonde hair. He had grown up in the area. The mind is extraordinary in its ability to create narrative from coincidence.

I had once interviewed serial killers. I had sat across from men who had done unspeakable things. I had learned to scan for darkness.

And now, instead of scanning danger to survive,

I was scanning love.

This chapter is not really about whether he murdered anyone.

It is about this:

I did not know how to tolerate stability.

When something begins to root,

when something begins to feel real,

the nervous system that grew up in volatility begins to itch.

It begins to look for the crack.

If there is no crack,

it will invent one.

I told myself it was intellectual curiosity.

Journalistic instinct.

Psychological acuity.

But beneath that was something more primitive.

If he is dangerous,

then my anxiety is justified.

If he is a killer,

then I can leave without humiliation.

*If he is dark,*

*then myth returns.*

Because here is the truth I did not see at the time:

Ordinary affection frightened me more than imagined monstrosity.

Monstrosity I knew how to navigate.

I had sat with it.

Flirted with it.

Studied it.

But a man who simply wanted me?

A man who was present?

A man who was human?

That required something far more terrifying.

Relaxation.

So, I began to construct danger.

Not consciously.

Not maliciously.

But systematically.

This is what attachment trauma does when intimacy deepens: It searches for proof that safety is an illusion.

The mind says, "He might have killed someone."

What it really means is, "This might not last."

And what that really means is, "I cannot survive another collapse." So better to create catastrophe than to wait for abandonment.

Better to expose darkness than to be blindsided by ordinariness.

When I finally told him my suspicion; that perhaps he had murdered his wife, perhaps he had committed the Derry killings it sounds absurd.

It was absurd.

But psychologically, it was perfect.

I was escalating the myth again.

*If he is capable of murder, then this is epic.*

*If he is epic, then this is not banal.*

*If this is not banal, then I am not small.*

Underneath the theatre was something much simpler:

I could not bear the thought that love might simply be gentle.

*Gentle did not feel sacred.*

*Gentle felt temporary.*

And so, I reached again for the archetype of predator.

Because predator at least guarantees voltage.

Even if it destroys me.

This chapter is not madness. It is hypervigilance meeting hope. It is a woman who has sat with killers, now unable to sit still with calm. It is the nervous system preferring catastrophe to vulnerability.

And it is the first clear sign that myth was still regulating me. Because if there is always a monster in the room,

I never have to risk being seen as ordinary.

When myth begins to soften, I reintroduce danger. That keeps the emotional temperature high. That keeps me in familiar territory.

The question now becomes:

Does he begin to pull away after this?

Or does he remain steady?
Because if he remains steady,
the destabilisation will shift location.
And that is where the real unravelling begins.

# Chapter Twelve – Away Day.

Hellebore (Lenten Rose) *The hellebore blooms in frost, a defiant miracle. Poisonous if touched too long; beauty that warns you not to stay.*

She turned to the window. Beyond the misted glass, the countryside unfurled in muted greens and browns, fields partitioned by ancient stone walls, low clouds pressing down like a secret. A sense of disquiet stirred in her belly, just beneath the thrum of joy.

The coach rattled along the wet roads, a low hum of tyres on asphalt mingling with the soft sigh of wind against the windows.

She pressed her forehead lightly to the glass, watching the countryside blur past in muted greens and greys, woodland giving way to fields, fields giving way to occasional farmhouses, the sprawl of small villages that smelled faintly of peat and rain.

The rhythmic rocking of the bus was hypnotic, a lull that should have calmed her, but instead it made her heart beat faster, her mind wandering into shadows she did not entirely want to follow.

Robert would be waiting in Tyrone when she got off.

That thought made her pulse quicken, a mixture of anticipation and unease curling inside her chest. She tried to remember the night in Belfast, the way he had leaned in close on the settee, the warmth of his hand brushing hers, the easy laughter, the weight of him beside her. And yet, alongside that memory came an unexpected edge, a hint of fear that prickled her skin.

His dead wife's voice flickered at the edges of her mind, a whisper threading through her thoughts. Was she imagining it, or had Serafina somehow managed to leave a trace of warning? The way Robert had laughed about the number plate on his car, the way he had tilted his head with that almost shy intensity; could that mask something darker? A chill crept along her spine.

She closed her eyes for a moment, and the images came unbidden: news footage, years old now, flickering in memory.

The bus slowed as it neared the station in Tyrone. She clutched her bag a little tighter, letting her knuckles press into the leather. The world outside was wet, shimmering with the sheen of rain, and the low hum of distant traffic reminded her that she was moving toward something unknown, toward him, toward the weekend that promised warmth and danger in equal measure.

He was there, standing under the small shelter of the station, coat collar turned up against the drizzle. Even at a distance, she recognised the way he carried himself; deliberate, measured, calm and yet she could see the edge in his eyes, the hint of intensity that had both thrilled and unsettled her from the beginning.

The walk across the wet carpark felt long, each step measured against the soft patter of rain. She approached the car, noticing the subtle weight of it, the same blue as before, the polished surface catching the grey light. The 666 on the number plate gleamed faintly, a small reminder of the odd, almost ritualistic quirks that made him simultaneously intriguing and unsettling.

He opened the door for her, a polite but deliberate gesture, and she slid into the passenger seat. The interior smelled faintly of leather and something else, faintly smoky, like a fire smouldering in the distance. He started the engine, and the hum of it seemed louder than the drizzle outside, as if it amplified the thoughts in her own head.

The drive through the woodland was hypnotic. Trees lined the road like silent sentinels, leaves slick and dark in the rain, branches brushing against each other with soft, sighing whispers.

Every shadow seemed to twist, every bend in the road felt deliberate, a prelude to something unseen. Her pulse quickened, partly from excitement, partly from unease. She tried to focus on the rhythm of the windshield wipers, on the muted colours of moss and bark and wet earth, but her thoughts circled inevitably back to him, to Serafina, to the news reports she had seen, to the warnings she imagined pressing against her mind like cold fingertips.

She glanced at him, caught in the pale light from the dashboard, and noticed the way his jaw was set, the careful stillness of his hands on the wheel.

A shiver ran down her spine. He had seemed safe in Belfast, even comforting, but now, in the quiet, dimly lit car, in the soft murmur of the rain, he felt like something more complex, more dangerous. Something capable of secrets that could bend her understanding of him into shadows she was not prepared for.

The road wound on, the trees opening occasionally to reveal glimpses of the distant hills, mist curling along the valleys. She felt the tension tighten and loosen in waves, a physical reminder that desire and fear often travelled hand in hand.

And she realised, with a shiver of both dread and thrill, that this weekend in Bettystown was not just a weekend. It was a journey into unknown territory, a test of intuition, courage, and the strange alchemy of attraction and danger.

The hotel rose out of the damp evening like something half remembered, its stone darkened by rain, windows glowing softly with lamplight. She felt a strange tightening in her chest as they pulled into the gravel drive, tyres crunching, the sound echoing too loudly in the quiet. She had been here before. The knowledge landed in her body before it reached her mind, a sudden awareness that unsettled her balance. Another man. Another time. Another version of herself.

Robert parked and turned off the engine. The silence that followed felt weighted, as though the car itself were listening.

He glanced at her, his expression unreadable, and she wondered whether he knew. Whether he could sense it in her posture, in the way her breath had shifted, the faint hesitation before she opened the door.

Inside, the air was warm and faintly perfumed with polish and old fabric. The carpet muted their footsteps, a deep red that seemed to absorb sound, and she felt as though they were walking through a held breath. At the reception desk, the woman smiled politely, keys exchanged hands, names spoken aloud. Her name sounded strange to her own ears in that place, as if it belonged to someone else.

As they moved toward the stairs, she felt it again. A flicker of memory. The curve of the banister beneath her palm. The way the light fell across the wall at the turn of the corridor. The echo of laughter that was not his. She slowed, almost imperceptibly, and he noticed.

"You've been here before, haven't you."

It was not an accusation. It was worse. It was quiet, observational, edged with something that made her skin prickle. She nodded, feeling suddenly exposed, as though a private page had been lifted from her life without permission.

"A long time ago," she said, too quickly. The words tasted thin.

His jaw tightened, just slightly. She caught it, the micro-movement, the restraint. Jealousy flickered there, but not the boyish kind she had known before. This was heavier, possessive in a way that made her heart thud against her ribs.

She felt both chosen and judged, and the duality unsettled her.

The room was on the second floor. When he opened the door, the warmth enveloped them, carrying the faint scent of linen, old wood, and something floral that reminded her of pressed petals. The curtains were drawn back, revealing a view of the darkening hills, mist clinging low, the landscape softened into something almost unreal.

She set her bag down and stood for a moment, suddenly unsure of herself. The room seemed to hold her history, not just this visit but others, impressions layered like sediment. She could almost see herself there before, younger, laughing, unguarded, unaware of how quickly intimacy could curdle into consequence.

Robert moved behind her. She felt him before she heard him, the shift in the air, the proximity. His hand rested briefly on her shoulder, not quite a caress, not quite neutral. She stiffened without meaning to.

"You look like you've seen a ghost," he said lightly.

The words struck her with uncanny precision. Her mouth went dry.

Later, after dinner, when the wine had warmed her limbs and the conversation had softened into something almost ordinary, the sense of being watched returned. Not by him. By something else. *Seraphina?* She excused herself and went to the bathroom, turning on the light too quickly, half expecting to see another woman standing there.

She did not. And yet.

As she leaned toward the mirror, she noticed the way the steam from the shower earlier had left a faint blur across the glass. For a moment, the reflection wavered. Her face seemed to recede, and behind it, impossibly, another presence suggested itself. Pale skin. Eyes that held neither accusation nor comfort, only knowledge.

Serafina.

The name surfaced without invitation. Her heart hammered, and she gripped the edge of the sink, grounding herself in the cool porcelain. This was ridiculous, she told herself. Grief left traces. The dead haunted the imagination of the living. That was all.

And yet the sense of warning pressed closer, not dramatic, not theatrical, but intimate. As though someone were standing just behind her shoulder, breathing softly, urging her to pay attention.

When she returned to the room, Robert was sitting on the edge of the bed, sleeves rolled up, the lamp casting shadows across his face that sharpened his features. He watched her closely, too closely, as if tracking a thought, she'd not spoken aloud.

"You seem far away," he said.

She smiled, automatically. "Just tired."

He nodded, but she did not believe he accepted it.

Later, lying beside him, the weight of his body warm and solid against hers, she felt the familiar pull of desire threading through her fear. It was there again, that helplessness, the sense of being taken somewhere she could not entirely steer.

His touch was assured, unhurried, and she felt herself responding despite the tightening in her chest, despite the images that flitted at the edge of her mind.

Afterward, as he slept, she lay awake listening to the steady rhythm of his breathing. The room was dark now, the hills outside invisible, the world narrowed to the rise and fall of his chest and the quiet thrum of her own thoughts.

Her mind returned, unbidden, to old news footage. Not Tyrone this time. Derry. A different voice. A different year. The same careful language. Unsolved. Intelligent. Elusive. The image of a young man with long flowing blonde hair surfaced again, and she felt the cold recognition ripple through her body.

She turned her head slightly, studying his face in the low light. The shadows softened him, but they also obscured.

She wondered, not for the first time, how well one could ever truly know another person. How easily charm could coexist with secrecy. How often women mistook intensity for safety.

The thought settled in her chest like a stone.

Beside her, he shifted in his sleep, murmuring something unintelligible. She flinched, then chastised herself for it. This was madness. Projection. Fear dressed up as intuition.

And yet, as she finally closed her eyes, the last thing she felt was not comfort, but vigilance. A sense that she had crossed into a territory where desire no longer moved alone, where every tenderness carried a shadow, and where the past, hers and his, was beginning to speak in a language she would soon be forced to understand.

Morning arrived without ceremony. A thin, grey light crept through the gap in the curtains, settling on the room like dust. She woke before him, the unfamiliar bed stiff beneath her, the air faintly cold against her skin. For a moment she lay very still, listening. His breathing was slow, even, untroubled. That, more than anything, unsettled her.

She slipped out of bed and crossed to the window. Outside, the hills were softened by mist, their outlines blurred into something almost gentle. A different kind of quiet lived here, not the comforting hush of sleep but a watchful stillness, as though the land itself were withholding comment. She wrapped her arms around herself and tried to shake the residue of the night from her body.

Behind her, the bed shifted.

"You're awake early," he yawned.

The sound of his voice made her shoulders tighten before she could stop herself. She turned, forcing a smile, telling herself she was tired, nothing more. He sat up, hair rumpled, eyes already alert in a way that felt disproportionate to the hour.

"I never sleep well in hotels, he went on. Too many people passing through. Too many stories left behind."

The words landed oddly. She felt a small internal jolt, like a misstep on a stair. She laughed lightly, as if he had made a joke.

"I always like them, she said. They make me feel anonymous."

He watched her for a beat too long.

"Some people like anonymity because it means no one knows what they've done."

The room seemed to cool. She felt it in her throat first, a tightening, then lower, a faint nausea blooming beneath her ribs. She told herself she was reading into it, that tone was everything, that men said stupid things all the time without meaning them. And yet the remark did not dissipate. It hung there, suspended, waiting.

He smiled then, as if to soften it, as if aware he had gone somewhere he did not entirely mean to reveal.

"I'm joking," he said. "Don't look for subtext."

She nodded. Of course. That was her role, wasn't it. The woman who thought too much.

Breakfast was served in a low-ceilinged room off the main corridor, all polished wood and muted florals. The smell of coffee was strong, almost acrid, and the clatter of cutlery seemed unnaturally loud. She chose a seat by the window, positioning herself instinctively so she could see the door.

He noticed.

Nervous? he asked, lightly.

She shook her head. "I just like the light."

They ordered. She realised, as the waitress walked away, that she could not remember the last time she had felt hungry. Her stomach felt sealed, as though her body had decided that digestion was a luxury it could not currently afford.

As they waited, he spoke about the drive they would take later, the woods they would pass through, how quiet it would be once they were properly out of town. He described it with a kind of pleasure that made her skin prickle.

"You can go for miles without seeing anyone," he said. "People underestimate how easy it is to disappear out here."

Her hand tightened around her coffee cup. The heat burned slightly, grounding her.

"Disappear's a strong word," she said carefully.

He shrugged. "Same difference, really. If no one's looking for you. If you're some kind of loner who isn't missed."

There it was again. That faint sense of being nudged, not shoved. An invitation to notice. Or a test.

The food arrived. Eggs, toast, something fried that smelled heavier than it should have so early in the day. She stared at the plate as if it belonged to someone else. When she lifted her fork, her hand trembled, just perceptibly.

"You're very quiet this morning," he said.

She forced herself to eat some egg. The first mouthful was a struggle. She swallowed it too quickly, the texture wrong, her throat constricting as if rejecting it. Fear, she realized, had a taste. Metallic. Dry.

"I didn't sleep well," she said. "Hotels."

He smiled again, but there was something else beneath it now. A watchfulness. As though he were cataloguing her responses, noting the places she faltered.

"Funny," he said. "I slept like a stone."

That did it. The calm certainty of it. The way he said it without irony, without qualification. She felt suddenly absurd for sitting there, for eating breakfast with a man she'd only just begun to know, for letting her imagination outrun her reason. And yet the feeling didn't retreat.

She finished the meal mechanically, each bite an act of will. Around them, other guests murmured, cups clinked, a radio played softly in the background. Ordinary life continued, oblivious.

When they stood to leave, he reached for her coat, holding it open for her. The gesture was courteous, intimate. As she slipped her arms into the sleeves, she felt the familiar pull toward him, the desire that had not diminished, only complicated itself.

"Thank you," she said.

He smiled, close now, his voice low.

"Careful," he said. "It's cold out. But I know you're terrifically warm blooded."

She laughed, because that was what one did. But as they walked back into the grey morning, the words echoed behind her eyes, rearranging themselves into something that no longer sounded like a joke at all.

The car was colder than she expected. Not unpleasantly so, just enough to make her aware of her skin, the thinness of her coat, the way the seatbelt crossed her chest like a deliberate line.

He adjusted the mirrors before starting the engine, precise, almost ceremonial, as though the order of things mattered deeply to him.

They pulled out of the hotel car park and onto the road without speaking.

Morning had not fully decided what it wanted to be. The sky was a pale, undecided grey, the light flat and diffuse, offering no shadows sharp enough to read. Fields stretched out on either side, winter-lean and quiet, hedgerows slick with damp. The radio came on briefly; some low, melancholy guitar, a man singing about loss and then he switched it off again.

"Too distracting," he said sharply.

The silence that followed felt intentional.

The road narrowed as they left the town behind, asphalt giving way to something older, more intimate. Trees closed in, their branches knitting together overhead, forming a tunnel of bare limbs and lichen-dark bark. The tyres hissed softly against the damp surface. Every so often, gravel crackled beneath them, a small, sharp sound that made her flinch despite herself.

"You've been here before," he said.

It wasn't a question.

She looked at him. His eyes stayed on the road.

"Derry?" she said after a beat. "A long time ago."

"Murders took place here; ohh many years ago."

"I know."

"Stupid me; I forgot who I was with ....Miss Psychotherapist, serial killer Queen."

She nodded. "They found the bodies further out; on the beach."

He smiled faintly, but it didn't reach his eyes.

"Funny," he said. "I always think places remember things like that. As if the land keeps a record of horror, even when people move on and forget."

The trees thickened. Light thinned. The car seemed suddenly very small within the corridor of wood and earth.

"I don't believe that," she said, though her voice lacked conviction.

"No?" He paused, then added softly, "I think dead girls leave impressions."

Her breath caught, just slightly.

'Are you ok, Chrissy?"

He glanced at her then, just for a second. The look was unreadable; not cruel, not kind; simply intent.

The Glen appeared suddenly, the trees breaking apart to reveal water lying flat and dark, a dull mirror under the sky. Mist hovered just above the surface, moving almost imperceptibly, like breath. He slowed the car but did not stop.

He drove on, past the turn-off, the lake slipping out of view as though it had never been there at all.

A pressure built behind her eyes. She felt the old, unwelcome instinct rise; the urge to placate, to smooth, to keep things calm. To be good. She hated that part of herself and yet it surfaced faithfully, every time.

"You're quiet again," he said.

"I'm thinking."

"About what?"

She chose her words carefully. About how quickly things can feel different.

"About the Derry murders."

The road began to climb, winding upward now, the forest thinning into scrub and rock. From here, the land opened into wide, empty stretches, the kind that made distance feel elastic. No houses. No people. Just the car, the road, the sound of the engine pulling steadily forward.

She heard her voice as if it were inside of her own head; *Killer, killer, he's a killer, run run run.* It was Serafina – trying to warn her.

She felt a sudden, sharp clarity; not panic, not yet; but awareness. The sensation of being inside a moment that would later return to her, uninvited, with perfect detail. The colour of the sky. The smell of damp earth. The cadence of his voice.

The car crested the hill. Ahead of them, the road disappeared into another long curve, the landscape opening into something vast and exposed. She sat very still, her body understanding before her mind allowed it to name the feeling.

This, she knew with a certainty that settled deep in her bones that this was the point of no return for the weekend.

And as the car carried them onward, deeper into the quiet, she realized she was no longer wondering whether she should trust him.

Serafina was inside if her head now.

A voice. Not real; but not imagined, either.

"I should never have drunk the tea," the voice whispered.

"He said it was chamomile. But the way he watched me... like he was waiting for it to take effect."

She blinked hard. Tried to dismiss it.

But the memory returned, more vivid now; the dream she'd had the night before.

Serafina in her wedding dress, pale as paper, standing at the foot of their bed, her hair tied in a soft bun, lips barely moving.

"He put something in my drink."

She had sat up in the dark, breath shallow, and felt a pressure in the room that wouldn't leave.

Now, in the car, she glanced sideways. Robert was humming tunelessly, tapping the steering wheel in time to nothing. There was something distant about him. Something curtained off.

"I was thinking..." she began slowly, "Maybe we should go back?"

He didn't reply.

She looked down at her lap. "You okay?"

He made a vague sound in his throat, like someone clearing dust. "Just tired."

She nodded. But her gut was tight now. A breath caught somewhere between her heart and lungs.

The night before, Serafina's voice had said one more thing.

"Have you seen the program about Robert's crimes?"

The BBC documentary.

The Derry Girls Murders.

Three girls. 1990's. Unsolved.

The killer was described by a witness: a teenager with long, pale hair. Maybe seventeen. Quiet. With cold eyes.

And Robert; only yesterday; had laughed when he said, "Back then I had hair down to my arse. Blonde, too. My mother said I looked like one of the feckin' Procul Harem."

It had been a throwaway comment. But now it looped in her mind.

Blonde hair. Seventeen. 1990's.

She closed her eyes and swallowed.

Serafina said inside of her head, "You think you're safe, but you're not. You'll wake up with blood all around your mouth and dead like me after drinking poison."

Her stomach clenched, not from nausea, but from something ancient: fear lodged in a woman's bones.

He turned toward her as they slowed for a roundabout.

"You're very quiet, love."

She smiled, lips trembling slightly. "Just tired," she echoed.

Inside, her instincts were screaming.

The second hotel was only thirty minutes away now. He'd booked it without asking her, said it was a surprise. It had once been a grand Georgian manor, now turned boutique seaside getaway. She should have been delighted.

But the closer they got, the more the air felt... wrong. Off.

Something in her kept replaying that moment in his flat, weeks earlier.

When he'd stood in the doorway watching her sleep.

She'd opened her eyes and caught him; just staring.

His face unreadable. Like he didn't recognise her. Or like he was deciding something.

"Have you ever been to Derry before?" he asked suddenly.

She shrugged. "I told you - a few times. Nice place. Quiet."

Serafina's voice returned again, cold and clear:

*You'll never make it back home.*

And then another memory; this one real.

He once told her, offhandedly, that his first dog had disappeared when he was little. "Vanished," he said. "One minute there, next minute gone. Like it never existed."

The car turned off the main road, down a smaller country lane, high hedges on either side. Trees closed in. A hawk passed overhead, casting a flash of shadow across the bonnet.

*Get out now,* said Serafina, from the back of her mind.

*You'll never get another chance to survive.*

Her hand was trembling now.

She faked a smile. "Can we stop? I feel sick. Just need a minute to breathe."

He frowned. "We're almost there."

"Please," she said. "Please. Just pull over."

A pause. Then he signalled, pulling into a lay-by near a crumbling old gate. The sea was just visible through the trees beyond.

She opened the door and stepped out, heart hammering. Rain spattered on her shoulders. She clutched her coat closed, took a shaky breath.

"Don't go too far," he called from the car. "There's no signal out here."

She nodded. And walked.

And walked faster.

And then ran.

She didn't stop until she reached the main road again, flagged down a passing lorry. She lied to the driver. Said her boyfriend was drunk. That she needed to get back to Belfast.

By nightfall, she was on the ferry.

By sunrise, she was in London.

By midday, she was staying with friend.

Alone. Alive and ....Pregnant.

Letters had come for her; texts and notes all passed to her by the owners of her rented house in Belfast.

*I was so jealous, I thought you'd been to the Hotel before with a lover. I'm sorry. I was moody. Forgive me; it's just I do love you very much, Robert.*

***

**Author's Notes:**

Hellebore; The Frost That Burns

Hellebore blooms in frost. A defiant miracle. Poisonous if handled too long. Beauty that warns you not to stay.

I knew something had shifted before I even reached him.

On the bus from Belfast, I felt it; that low metallic taste in the mouth, that prickle along the ribs. The kind of dread that does not announce itself but settles quietly, like mist.

I told myself it was nerves.

Excitement.

Love.

It wasn't.

When I saw him, he was already somewhere else.

Not absent; worse. Present, but withdrawn. A stillness that felt like something bracing for impact. His jaw set. His eyes flat.

He said nothing was wrong.

That's the most destabilising sentence in the world.

Nothing is wrong.

When everything in your body knows something is.

We drove.

The trees blurred past like silent witnesses. The sky was low and swollen with rain. I remember the sound of tyres on wet tarmac and the feeling that every bend in the road was leading us somewhere we could not return from.

He asked if I had been to the hotel before.

I said yes.

A long time ago.

The words felt thin, brittle.

He thought I had taken another man there.

He thought I had a history he wasn't allowed to touch.

Jealousy in him didn't look like pleading.

It looked like cold.

And once before, when he had been angry, he had struck my leg; not enough to bruise the bone, but enough to mark the air between us. Enough that my nervous system had filed it under: danger.

So, when the silence thickened in that car, I was not thinking about romance.

I was thinking about survival.

But I also loved him.

That is the part that makes it unbearable.

I loved the man in the glen.

The man who had taken me into the circle of trees.

The man who had said I came like sunlight into a dark room.

And now here he was beside me, rigid with suspicion, jealousy tightening his voice.

Two versions of the same man.

I did not know how to hold both.

We arrived at the hotel.

It should have been beautiful.

Instead, everything felt brittle.

We moved around each other like strangers trying not to break something already cracked. There was no shouting. No cinematic explosion. Just tension, thin and sharp as glass.

Somewhere inside me, something shattered.

Not loudly.

Quietly.

Like a wine glass slipping from a table in the next room.

And I felt the child.

Not the child in my womb.

The child in me.

The one who had learned that when a man's mood turns cold, you disappear before it turns worse.

But there was also another child; the possibility of one.

Because I was pregnant.

And I knew it.

We could have been a family.

That is what makes this chapter hurt.

Not just the rupture.

The future that dissolved with it.

On that drive, in that room, I felt the story crack.

Not the novel.

The life.

We could have had a farmhouse.

A child running between fields.

Ordinary breakfasts.

Storms that passed and didn't end everything.

Instead, we had silence.

He later said he was jealous.

He later said he loved me.

He later apologised for the mood, for the suspicion.

But in that moment, I was already leaving.

By nightfall I was on a ferry.

By sunrise I was in London.

By midday I was somewhere else entirely.

Geographical flight is an art form when you've perfected it.

It feels decisive.

It feels sovereign.

It is also a way of not staying long enough to see whether something could repair.

The last time I saw him, he walked out of the hotel room.

There was no music.

No slow-motion understanding.

Just the ordinary click of a door closing.

I did not know it was the last time.

That is what haunts me.

If I had known, would I have said something different?

Would I have touched his face differently?

Would I have chosen repair over departure?

Years later, when I heard that Lady Gaga song — the one about not knowing it's the last time — it felt like a knife sliding neatly between memory and regret.

Because that's how it is.

The last time never announces itself.

It just passes.

And later, you replay it with the ache of someone who finally understands the weight of ordinary seconds.

We were two dysregulated nervous systems.

His jealousy tightening into coldness.

My fear accelerating into flight.

## THE PSYCHOLOGY OF FEAR OF LOVE

Neither of us knew how to stay inside rupture.
And so, the love story did not end in myth.
It ended in fracture.
In a hotel room.
In rain.
With a child forming quietly inside me.
That is darker than tragedy.
Because it is plausible.
It is almost ordinary.
And that is what makes it unbearable.

# SIX YEARS LATER.

# Chapter Thirteen: Charlie.

*Black Rose for the Heart That Could Not Stay: A flower bred in shadows; where love once bloomed and then withered into silence.*

In the summer in her rented London home, with its long back garden leading to the river, was a sanctuary for her and her six-year-old son, Charlie.

As Charlie frolicked in the blue paddling pool, creating make-believe countries with his toy animals, Chrissy immersed herself in quilting, knitting, or a good book, enjoying the blissful moments of shared conversation under the balmy sun.

As her beloved Charlie grew, their bond deepened through water fights and chess games by the summer fire. Laughter echoed in the living room as they engaged in playful banter. The love between mother and son was palpable, and as the fire crackled, Charlie, hot and sweaty, declared victory in their chess match, prompting a playful wrestling session.

With Charlie tucked into bed with a storybook, she, now alone in the silent rented St Margaret's house, grappled with the nagging feeling of loneliness.

Pouring herself a gin and tonic, she tried to relax but couldn't shake the looming dread.

The weight of financial worries as a single mother without support pressed on her, and nightmares of a Dickensian fate haunted her thoughts.

Despite financial constraints, her and Charlie found joy in free activities, from wintry daily walks in Richmond Park to summertime adventures in Isabella Plantation.

Their daily after-school picnics under a tree were filled with simple pleasures and the shared excitement of caterpillar hunts.

In the midst of life, she found friendship with Anne, the mother of movie star Sean Wiley. Their contrasting lives unfolded in Anne's stunning Sheen home; where lavish parties with celebrities were the norm. Anne, a beautiful and talented painter, was a source of both envy and fascination for Chrissy.

During one summer evening, Anne confronted her about her fear of intimacy and urged her to find love before it was too late.

As they lounged in the back garden, Anne shared insights from her favorite writer, Ramtha, about soulmates and the yearning for connection. Anne's encouragement to embrace love resonated, but Chrissy remained skeptical.

Their conversation drifted to Anne's glitzy, movie star lifestyle, her secret cigarettes, and her loving relationship with her husband, Chips. Anne's observations about her changing appearance and her need for love struck a chord, leading to a moment of vulnerability and self-reflection.

As the sun dipped below the horizon, Charlie interrupted their conversation with a paper plane, injecting a dose of childlike innocence into the grown-up dialogue. Anne, undeterred, continued to espouse the wisdom of finding one's soulmate.

Anne continued to scrutinise Chrissy, her green eyes piercing through the evening haze. The scent of overripe peaches mingled with the cool breeze, carrying with it the weight of unspoken truths and the echoes of a distant river.

As they settled back into conversation, Anne's tone shifted to a more serious note.

"Darling, you really must find a man."

Chrissy sighed; her gaze momentarily fixed on the distant horizon. "I don't want to; I'm too sad about it not working out between Robert and I."

Anne leaned in, my expression a mix of disbelief and genuine worry. "Are you sure you're, okay? What do you mean by not working out?"

She fidgeted, a sense of unease settling in. "I told him that I had met someone else and he asked me was it love and I said yes it was. I told him about Charlie and he said that we were a package and then nothing. I heard he was with another women. Someone called Jade."

Anne frowned and reached for a plate of snacks nearby. "Let's indulge a bit, shall we? Maybe some snacks will help clear the air."

The snacks were an assortment of gourmet delights Anne had generously bought with her; artisanal cheeses, olives stuffed with garlic, and crackers with a hint of rosemary from her local Waitrose.

As they nibbled on these treats, the conversation shifted back and forth between the peculiarities Anne's glamorous movie star peopled world. Only last week she had entertained Leonardo Di Caprio.

The weather played its part, alternating between warm bursts of sunshine and cool breezes. A sense of fragility hung in the air. Their clothes, too, reflected the contrast between Anne's chic Dior elegance and her more understated Tesco range attire.

As the sun dipped below the horizon, casting long shadows across the garden, the conversation deepened. Anne, always the provocateur, pressed on.

"You need to get a grip on reality."

Amidst the snacks, the changing weather, and the stylish enigma of their clothing, she grappled with the unsettling truth that her life lacked sexual love.

The river flowed quietly nearby, carrying with it the secrets and mysteries that seemed to envelop her like a shroud.

As the evening wore on and the warmth of the day lingered in the air, Anne reached for a chilled bottle of white wine.

Chrissy poured the crisp liquid into delicate glasses, the condensation forming droplets that glistened in the fading sunlight.

"Chrissy, you said you thought he was the Derry serial killer; that you were sure he'd killed his wife." Anne said, her concern evident in the furrow of her brow.

Chrissy took a sip of the refreshing wine and leaned back; her gaze fixed on the play of sunlight through the leaves.

"I know, Anne. But I did love him; I just ...I didn't know him and she...."

'Who's she?"

"No one! Anne, its ok, Charlie fills all my needs for love and cuddles."

Anne sighed, her fingers tracing the rim of her wine glass.

"Have you considered seeking professional help? Someone who can guide you through these complexities so you don't end up all alone!"

She hesitated, then nodded slowly. "I've thought about it. But the psychic, Mike Baker, told me that true love's kiss could break the chains and cure me. It sounds absurd, I know, but he said my Twin Flame would heal me and he's called J. I've searched Mike Baker up again online; but I can't find him."

Anne chuckled, the sound mingling with the soft rustle of leaves in the warm breeze. "True love's kiss? Life isn't a fairy tale. You need practical solutions, not whimsical notions."

"I know, Anne, but sometimes a little magic is all we need. And Mike also said something about meeting my Twin Flame, someone with the initial J. Maybe that's the key to unraveling all of this."

Anne raised an eyebrow, her skepticism evident.

"A Twin Flame named J? You can't hinge your entire existence on the whims of a psychic. It's time to take control of your life, find a marriage and stability."

"But what if he's right? What if there's someone out there who can truly understand me! My Twin Flame!" Chrissy mused, her fingers tracing patterns on the armrest of her chair.

Anne sighed, her gaze softening.

"Darling, I just want you to be happy and healthy. If seeking this J is what you believe will bring you peace, then go for it. Just promise me you won't lose yourself in the process."

As the sun dipped below the horizon, casting a warm glow over Dragonfly Villas, Anne and Chrissy lingered in conversation, the weight of the hot summer air pressing upon them. The river whispered its secrets, and the possibility of true love's kiss lingered in the air, a thread of hope in the tapestry of life.

Amidst the uncertainty, the scent of overripe peaches of her friend's perfume lingering in the air, she confronted the constant fear of being single forever that threatened to overshadow her life.

She found solace in the golden rays of the setting sun. She settled into a wrought-iron chair on the patio, a notepad in hand, and watched as Charlie continued his playful adventures in the expansive garden. The distant laughter of children, the gentle rustle of leaves, and the soothing hum of the river created a backdrop for contemplation.

The garden was warm and faintly humming; summer pressing its soft breath into every leaf. Hydrangeas puffed themselves up in blues and pinks along the borders, and Anne sat cross-legged on the old wooden bench, slicing pieces of apple with her penknife and passing them to Chrissy one at a time.

"I do think soulmates are real," Anne said, brushing her fringe back with the back of her wrist. "I mean, there are people who come into your life and just... rearrange the furniture, you know? But it's not about sex or marriage."

Chrissy half-smiled. "Recognition can be terrifying, though. What if you recognise something monstrous?"

Anne looked up. "Are we talking about Charlie's dad now?"

Chrissy didn't answer right away. She tilted her face toward the sun, as if she might disappear into it. "I was haunted," she said at last. "By his wife."

Anne blinked. "What do you mean, haunted?"

"I mean... I saw her. In the house. In the mirror. In the corners of my dreams. She'd whisper. And it was like she was sitting beside me, smoking and smiling bitterly, telling me that he'd poisoned her. That she'd died because of him."

A silence bloomed between them.

Chrissy swallowed. "We were on our way to Bettystown when it happened. For a moment it was beautiful. Until it wasn't and I became afraid; you know what I'm like' I have bad nerves."

Anne reached for her hand. "Bloody Hell."

"I thought... I thought he was the one who did the Derry murders, Anne. There was this programme. Long blond hair. A young man. Robert told me that he had long blond hair as a teenager. Sefarina told me it was him. I ran. I just ran."

They sat like that for a while, in the stillness, birds fluting faintly in the sycamores.

And then, the landline rang.

She stood, brushing grass off her trousers, and went inside. The kitchen was cool and dim after the garden. She picked up the phone, a sudden tightness in her throat.

"Hello?"

As the line clicked dead, Chrissy stood there, staring at the receiver, breath shallow.

Outside, the garden was bathed in gold. Anne had gone.

And suddenly, in the silence of the house, she felt something. A ripple. A curl of soundless laughter, cold as moonlight. A woman's voice; not in her ears, but in the dark centre of her bones.

She turned and stared at the wall, the ceiling, the corner of the kitchen. Serafina was gone. But the echo of her was not.

And yet; beneath that, deeper still was grief. For the man she'd fled. For the child who would never know his father. But she had to be safe and keep her son safe.

She walked back out into the garden. The apple slices lay untouched on the bench. The bees moved lazily between flowers. The world didn't care about ghosts.

But she did.

She sat down, and for a long time, she didn't move.

***

**Author's Clinical Notes:**

Six years later I was in a rented house in London with a six-year-old boy and a life that did not resemble the one I had imagined in the glen.

I will call him Charlie.

Charlie had soft hair and a serious face when he concentrated. He would sit on the floor lining up toy cars while I stood in the kitchen calculating rent in my head.

I was a mother.

And still unrooted.

That is a particular kind of ache.

Not tragic.

Not dramatic.

Just a low, constant hum of impermanence.

I spoke to my friend Anne about twin flames.

I still believed, somewhere in me, that there was a man whose initial began with J.

A psychic had once said it. I had built entire emotional scaffolding around that letter.

Anne looked at me in a way that was neither cruel nor indulgent.

"What about stability?" she asked. "You're in rented. You're hinging your existence on the whim of a psychic. Can't you find something solid?"

But I wasn't chasing fantasy for entertainment.

I was chasing recognition.

"What if it's right?" I said. "What if there is someone who truly understands me?"

What I meant was:

What if there is someone who makes me feel real?

Anne said something I didn't understand at the time.

"I think soulmates exist," she said. "But they're not necessarily the ones you marry. They come to rearrange the furniture. They don't always stay."

Rearrange the furniture.

That's what Robert had done.

He hadn't built the house.

He'd moved the walls.

And the problem was this:

I still felt like a ghost in my own life.

Six years later.

I was functioning.

Working.

Mothering.

But I did not feel fully inhabited.

In relationships, I had always felt slightly outside the frame. Slightly unreal. Like an actress in someone else's domestic scene.

And when I looked at other women; the ones who seemed grounded in kitchens and school runs and shared mortgages; I felt transparent beside them.

Not inferior.

Unreal.

That is worse.

Because you cannot compete with reality when you do not feel embodied.

This is where the theme becomes unavoidable.

The book is not about Robert.

It is not about jealousy.

It is not even about myth.

It is about freezing.

I froze in childhood when embodiment equalled danger.

I thawed in flashes; in forests, in voltage, in sex that felt mythic.

And then I froze again when rupture came.

Six years later, I was still partially frozen.

Functioning does not mean unfrozen.

Motherhood did not automatically anchor me.

Rent did not make me root.

Time did not dissolve the ghost.

I was haunted not just by Serafina; not just by the idea of the wife; but by a version of myself that had once felt briefly alive.

The woman in the glen.

The woman under hail.

The woman who believed she could be chosen.

That woman felt like fiction.

And so, I clung to twin flame language.

Because if there was still a J somewhere,
if destiny was merely delayed,
then my life had not narrowed into rent and routine.

# Sixteen Years Later.

# Chapter Fourteen: Twin Flame J.

*Yellow Roses for the Flame That Could Not Burn: Joyful on the surface, but born of longing; the colour of what never quite was.*

In the midst of July, 2025, raindrops played upon the window of Chrissy's rented London flat, slow and then fast, escalating into a breezy, fragrant summer storm. She put on her coat and went out the front door and into her car and headed for Kew.

Many years had passed since Mike the psychic had foretold the arrival of her Twin Flame, J.

Kew Gardens unfolded its botanical wonders under the relentless embrace of the sun. The air was thick with the intoxicating fragrance of blooming flowers and the lively hum of bees.

Mike had tracked her down on Facebook after one of his clients had read her memoir where she had mentioned him by name.

They both strolled along the vibrant beds of multi-coloured blooms, her senses heightened by the kaleidoscope of colours and the warmth that enveloped them both.

They decided to meet in Kew Gardens, a place resonating with life, much like their own intertwining destinies. And as they sat face to face in Kew's quaint café, she bit into a cheese baguette, the warmth of the day mingling with the bittersweet emotions of seeing Mike again.

She stirred sugar into hot tea, sighing as she reflected on the journey Mike had set her on so many years ago; the quest for a Twin Flame named J.

"Mike, I love you to bits, but you really started me off on a journey, and now I'm getting old," she confessed, her gaze wandering over the vibrant landscape. "I've grey hair, for God's sake; my son is twenty-two years of age! Where the hell is my Twin Flame...this J you told me about all those years ago!"

Mike listened, his eyes reflecting a mixture of compassion and understanding. The sun's rays cast a gentle glow on their conversation, adding a touch of warmth to the complexities that unfolded.

'A friend of mine told me about you, you wrote about me in your memoir.... and so flatteringly that I decided to track you down on Facebook. What a blast from the past you are! I didn't forget you! I read your byline in the newspapers, followed your journalistic career in the Sunday Times!'

'Thankyou! I worked hard. Work was all I had. No relationships – not since his father. I devoted myself to looking after my boy. He's twenty-two can you believe it!"

'Unbelievable! I saw photos of him on your Instagram and what a fine-looking young man! You must be so proud!"

"I think a search for meaning in life took over from my search for J; or maybe I got them both confused?" Chrissy continued, the weight of years and unfulfilled dreams evident in her words. "Aren't I supposed to be able to see and feel my own Twin Flame?"

Mike took a sip of his team, leaned back in his chair and replied, 'Chris, what would you say to J if you ever caught up with him?'

Chrissy laughed. 'Why, I'd tell him I loved him, Mike; of course I would. I'd live happily ever after!'

***

As they meandered through the garden, the air thickened with the scent of blooming flowers, and the distant sounds of laughter and birdsong created a poignant backdrop to their conversation.

Now caught in the rain of memories, Chrissy shared the untold story of her life that Mike had missed.

The light rain became a symphony, washing away life's regrets. The lush greenery of Kew Gardens became witness to a chapter in the unfolding saga of their intertwined lives. As the summer storm grew wetter, she turned to Mike, stress etching lines on her pale face.

Mike touched her shoulder gently.

"Chrissy.' Mike's eyes held a profound depth as they delved into her soul. "You've had a child, you bought him up all alone and you've done so very well," he gently reminded her.

"I know," she replied, her voice carrying the weight of unspoken stories.

"He's the love of your life."

"Yes, yes, he is. My Charlie, my very own Angel."

They walked on and lingered in the wood cabin built near the lake where they sheltered out of the rain.

"Though, Mike: I wanted to try that thing; you know, lovemaking like you see in the movies, amazing lovemaking – lovemaking like the Gods. Emerald Fennell's Wuthering Heights. Cathy and Heathcliff! Breath-taking passion! Yeah, to love-make like the Gods of nature." She gazed around her at the beauty of the wildness of nature and grinned.

Mike's gaze lingered on her, a silent witness to the unfulfilled desires of her heart.

"When was the last time you made love, Chris?" he asked, his tone carrying a mixture of compassion and curiosity.

"Twenty-two years ago, with Robert, my son's father," she confessed, 'Or is it twenty-three?"

Her narrative unfolded, painting a poignant picture of single motherhood.

The summer rain, a constant companion to their conversation, intensified. Its rhythmic patter became a backdrop to her recollections of another time, another place – Gortin Glen in Ireland, where the air was heavy with the scents of earth, wet foliage, and the distant promise of rain.

In the vivid tapestry of her memories, Gortin Glen emerged as a sanctuary, a ring of trees forming a natural haven.

One hot and balmy afternoon, Chrissy and her son's father, Robert sought refuge within this sacred circle; a ring of trees in a complete circle. The forest embraced them as they lay down, shedding inhibitions along with their clothes until they were naked on the floor of the wood in the very centre. It was more like a ritual than lovemaking. It was how they had made their son that wet Thursday afternoon in April 2003.

As she recounted the moments, each detail became a brushstroke on the canvas of a long past love.

Robert pounded her into the ground as if trying to make her one with the earth; taking part in a sacred ritual to make a child. Hail had come down in huge white stones and they stood naked in the trees like two fauns and watched the storm in awe of it.

Suddenly, amidst the tumult, a rainbow graced the sky, a celestial witness to their passion and the sun miraculously emerged.

"We stepped out of the ring of the woods inside of the Gortin Glen. According to the doctors, I was infertile," Chrissy shared with Mike, her words spoken against the backdrop of a sun-lit rain-soaked Kew Gardens.

Chrissy thought back to the scene in the wood all of those years ago recalling her lover's words.

'What would you call it if we made a child?'

"Cloud," she whispered, gazing at the sky adorned with drifting clouds.

'Do you know, I think that you would!'

A laughter, a promise, hung in the air as they embarked on a journey down to the lake, a place believed to cure infertility. Buck naked, they waded into the freezing lake, laughter bubbling up like the water around them. The shining April heat, though unexpected, draped the scene with a surreal silvery warmth. Back on land, they indulged in the intimacy of their connection, the forest bearing witness to their utter vulnerability. The aroma of wet earth mingled with the sounds of the gushing waterfall, creating a sensory symphony that echoed through the forest.

Larches, tall and majestic, framed the lovers in a delicate dance of shadows. The air hummed with the promise of renewal as they both lay naked and intertwined.

"I've just had a premonition that we've just now made a son! But you'll never set eyes on him. Not. Ever," Chrissy prophesied.

Robert frowned, 'Why would something like that ever happen?'

Gortin Glen, with its lush greenery and enchanting ambiance, tall trees stood like guardians, their leaves forming a verdant canopy that filtered the dappled sunlight. Those days in that balmy early summer that year were filled with the sweet fragrance of blooming flowers and the earthy scent of moss-covered rocks. The magic of Gortin Glen seemed to weave its enchantment, kindling a flame that grew with every step. They came to a river and lay naked on the rocks beside it. Robert's lips met hers in a tender kiss, the heatwave making them both giddy and thirsty and wanderers amidst the ancient guardians of the forest. Time seemed to stand still as they embraced the magic of the glen, their connection deepening with each heartbeat. Their laughter echoed through the glen, harmonising with the song of birds and the rustling leaves. They swam in the warm water, came out and lay on hot rockery.

Robert, gazing into her eyes, felt the depth of their connection. "Christine, it feels like time stands still here, doesn't it?"

"It's like we're in our own world."

"Chrissy, there's something I need to tell you. I love you. More than I thought was ever possible."

"I... I care about you a lot. But you were married before. Do you still love your ex-wife?"

"Chris, what Serafina and I had is in the past. I care for you in a way I've never cared for anyone else. I want us to create something beautiful together."

"I'm just scared. Scared that I'll never be enough, that I'll always be compared to her and fall short. If you died now and went to heaven and so did I ...who would you go to, Serafina ....or to me?"

"Chrissy, you, of course I'd go to you! You're so special it hurts; you're unique, and I love you for who you are. My past is just that; a past. What matters is our present and the future we can build together with our child."

"I want to believe that.'

Shadowy silver fish slid through the brown gloom of the stream; green weeds motionless. She watched curiously as he went back and forth, this man who was so wild and raw and in touch with nature. Chrissy glanced up at the foreboding of a sky turning bruise purple with the threat of rain. He lay in her lap and she stroked his lovely silky dark hair.

That day; the world seemed to hold its breath. The forest slowed, its rhythms gentler, its stillness sacred. The weather went crazy and snowflakes fell like whispers, each one a tiny, intricate miracle, vanishing as they kissed the earth. Berries hung from branches, glistening like jewels, while pine needles swayed softly, their fronds catching shafts of golden light that poured through the canopy above.

They stood, shivering and stripped bare, they made love on the forest bed, within the ring; a circle where the veil between our world and theirs felt thinner. The trees were alive, their bark rough yet pulsing with life, as though they had seen eternity and would still stand when all else fell.

He laughed, a sound that seemed to harmonise with the nature around them. 'You know, I think you would. Go and bathe in the lake, Chris. It cures infertility. Go on ahead.'

They waded buck naked into the freezing lake, the cold water a sharp contrast to the warmth of the day. Emerging giggling, she lay next to him, the water droplets on her skin glistening in the sunlight.

She lay on top of him, brushing her mouth against the skin on his sun-warmed back to dry herself. The sound of the waterfall gushing down loudly in the background created a natural symphony. The heat bore down heavily, but the coolness of the forest provided relief.

Tiny rabbits hopped delicately through the underbrush. Larches towered over them, their branches forming a pattern of dark lace against the sky. Water trickled into the cool brown stream near where they lay, the sound reminiscent of rain on rain. She blinked at the sky.

It was Easter, April, not really summer at all, yet it was so gorgeously, sexily hot.

She lay on him, and he turned, making love to her again.

'Come here and live with me, baby,' he whispered, his voice husky with emotion.

'Maybe,' she replied.

He went down on her in the heat, the scent of pine filling the air. A soft, warm summer breeze caressed her skin.

Then, he looked deathly pale, his skin whiter than chalk. A tiny stream of blood poured out of her onto the blanket. He sat up, concern etching his features. 'You're bleeding? Is it...?'

'Oh God, I should have got dressed,' she said, embarrassment flooding her. 'It's so embarrassing. I'm sorry, Robert. It's my period.'

'Don't worry. Doesn't matter. It's natural.'

The April sky had turned a delicious slate silver. The water lay still, not a flicker of a breeze. Robert bathed her tenderly with water from the stream, gently pressing wet tissue into the folds of her body to soak up the blood loss.

He cleaned her repeatedly with the cool stream water. Shadowy silver fish slid through the brown gloom of the stream; green weeds remained motionless.

She watched curiously as he went back and forth, his tenderness a balm to her embarrassment. She looked up at the sky, now turning bruise purple with the threat of rain. He lay in her lap, and she stroked his lovely dark hair. 'I've just had a premonition that we've just now made a son! But you'll never set eyes on him.'

***

Back in present day in Kew, the July rain had subsided, leaving a glistening sheen on the leaves, and the air was thick with the scent of wet earth and blossoms.

She turned to Mike: "The next time we met was the trip to the Hotel in Bettystown and our argument and I ran back to London."

As they both wandered through Kew Garden's botanical haven, they found themselves in the rose garden, where velvety petals shimmered with raindrops. The air was thick with the heady sensual perfume of roses, and the colours ranged from delicate pink pastels to deep lusty reds.

Mike touched her hand. "Women that have been sexually abused often can't ever trust anyone. It's such a terrifying and deep betrayal. They often end up all alone. You've spent your entire life seeking healing; even studying serial killers in person whose lives were destroyed by adoption; who were made monsters. You're now a qualified psychotherapist; yet only now finding your wholeness; through self-healing. Healing those who have suffered like you have."

The heat was un-English; the kind that shimmered off paving like a spell. Kew Gardens pulsed with it: sap rising under bark, lily-pond water thick as breathing, the whole afternoon heavy with magnolia perfume and the slow throb of cicadas. Beyond the great Palm House, Chrissy and Mike had wandered deep into the quieter acreage; past the Chinese golden larches, past avenues of atlas cedar; until they reached the redwood grove where the air changed, resin-cool beneath trunks older than any of their sorrows.

Mike stopped, tilting his face to the filtered sun. "Here," he said, voice soft as moss. "This is a good place. Tell me what's weighing on you."

Chrissy clutched her sun-hat against a hot up-draft. "Some huge things have happened," she managed. "I've never told anyone else. I'm so deeply ashamed."

Mike's eyes—sea-grey, kind—held hers. "You can tell me anything."

She set her bag on a root, drew a slow breath scented with redwood sap and distant rose-oil from the summer beds. "I can speak to ghosts," she began, almost choking on the admission. "For six years Serafina—Robert's dead wife—has haunted me. She whispered that Robert was a killer, that he poisoned her, that he was the one behind the Derry murders. I believed her."

Wind stirred the canopy; traceries of light slid over Mike's linen shirt. "Invisible liars," he murmured.

Chrissy nodded, voice trembling. "I didn't know that term then. And I... I rang Robert's family. He hasn't spoken to his brother in decades, but I found the number.

His brother's wife—Maggie—called me back." She swallowed. "Maggie told me Serafina died of natural causes. Toxicology clear. Then I asked—God, I sounded mad—'Did Serafina suspect Robert in the Derry murders?'

Maggie laughed. Said it was preposterous. Said Serafina had been madly in love with him—would have done anything to keep him—and if she were a ghost, she'd tear apart any new woman he loved."

Chrissy's hands shook. "That was the moment I knew: I'd been manipulated by a soul who loved on and who could blame her."

Mike exhaled slowly. "I thought you'd reach that knowing. The Spiritualist Church should have warned you: never trust the unseen unless it comes from a guide you've vetted with your whole soul." He tapped his heart. "That's how I knew you had a twin flame whose name began with J."

He studied her. "Tell me, Chrissy—haven't you met J yet, my Spirit Guide tells me that you know him."

Everything inside her folded. She dropped to her knees on the sun-baked mulch, tears springing hot as the day.

"I didn't know," she sobbed. "Not until we'd been long apart. Then I saw it on the child-support paperwork—Robert Joseph L."

Mike crouched, steadying her shoulders. The redwoods loomed like cathedral pillars around them, their bark cool against the oven-heat beyond. "Ask," he said gently. "Ask what you need."

"Mike—" Her voice broke. "Ask your spirit guide: is he the one?"

He closed his eyes, lips moving in silent conversation with something Chrissy could not see. A hush pressed in tree-breath, honeyed sap, distant lawn-mowers silenced for a heartbeat. Then he opened his eyes, light catching a fleck of gold in the grey.

"You're right," he said. "Robert Joseph L is your twin flame."

Mike rose, offering his hand. She let him pull her to her feet; heat radiated from the earth, coolness seeped from the trunks; hot and sharp, cold and smooth: the world's opposite textures meeting in her skin.

"Twin-flame love isn't a fairytale. It's a mirror. It shows every crack in your self-worth. You ran because you don't believe you're lovable, Chrissy. Your history taught you to mistrust devotion. Yes, you can accept your son's unconditional love, but a man's erotic devotion? You doubt you can hold it. That doubt colluded with Serafina's lies."

She looked up through the branches; the sky was a burning nickel coin. "So, what do I do now? He's with another woman."

Mike said simply. "A twin flame is different from usual love - volatile, profound. Some people can't bear that kind of heat."

Chrissy pressed a palm to the rough redwood bark. It felt ancient, forgiving. She pictured Robert's scarred knuckle on the gear stick, the blue-eyed smile that once lit her whole body.

"I thought ghosts told the truth," she whispered.

"Some do," Mike answered. "But some are just echoes of the living; carrying their jealousy, their fear; their love."

She closed her eyes.

When she opened her eyes, Mike had stepped back. Light filtered green-gold through redwood needles; the air smelled of earth after rain, though no rain had fallen.

Chrissy drew a breath that filled every narrow hallway of her lungs. And somewhere in the hush between two heartbeats, the ghost of Serafina fell silent.

"Christine," he said, gently, like he was handing her something made of spun glass, "you think that love is meant to look like the marriages you see around you. All those Sunday roasts and polite silences and separate bedrooms. But it isn't. That's endurance. That's social contract. Love—real love—is something else entirely."

He paused, eyes scanning the tree line where the wind was brushing through the beeches like a hymn.

"Love, the kind you're aching for, the kind you had, isn't unreal, Christine. It's not fiction. It is rare, yes—but not unreal. The reason we see it most often in films, in novels, in songs that nearly lift the soul out of our bodies, is because that's the only place it can fully breathe. We're not built for it anymore—not in the soft cages of modern life. We're only fit for lists and schedules. For bills and doing the recycling."

He shifted on the bench beneath the redwood canopy, his voice dipping lower, more thoughtful.

"Once, we were people who lit fires with our own hands. We hunted, we bled, we mourned under stars. Back then, the soul had somewhere to go; somewhere wild to burn. But now... we live domesticated lives. And we try to fit something elemental, like a storm, into something tame, like a teacup. It can't survive there. It dies, Christine. It folds in on itself."

He turned to her, looking straight through her to the centre of the ache she carried.

"Love like you had... it's not designed to stay. It's too bright. Too alive. It would burn your house down just to say it's home. That's why we see it in movies and books, and not in suburbia. Because those loves are meant to vanish. They show up to change you, not to stay. They are wild gods, and they don't do mortgages."

He leaned back, sighing through his nose like someone exhaling an old flame.

"But take heart. You had it. That thing most people only ever hear about in song lyrics or watch in the rain-slick close-ups of movie kisses. You felt it. It lived in you. It chose you to carry it, even if only for a moment. That's something. And Charlie – your son – he was born of it – that makes him very very special."

He looked at her, his voice soft as moss.

"So, when the storms come; when you hear that song that used to make you cry, or you smell something sharp like the cologne he wore, or you walk home in the dark and the rain feels like it used to; remember it. Let it stir in your bones. Let it hurt a little, because that's how you know it was real."

He held out a palm, like catching a snowflake.

"Love isn't something to own. It's something to be changed by. And you, Christine... you were changed. That's what matters." He gave her a small, crooked smile. "And if you're lucky... it'll come again. Maybe not the same shape. Maybe not with the same fire. But it'll come. And when it does; you'll recognise it. Because once you've been burned by real love, you can spot the heat a mile away."

Mike Baker died of cancer three weeks after Kew Gardens. May he rest in peace.

***

Mike was correct, they did create something beautiful together, who would live on past both of them. Even though he was never to meet or know their child; Chrissy called him Charlie Arthur Merlin.

***

**Author's Clinical Notes:**

There is one thing I see clearly now.

I mythologised the rupture.

Not because it wasn't painful.

But because I could not bear it being ordinary.

The ending of my relationship with Robert could have been understood as this:

Two dysregulated people.

*Jealousy.*

*Fear.*

*Flight.*

*Poor repair.*

*Timing.*

*Immaturity.*

Human.

But I elevated it.

*Twin flame.*

*Prophecy.*

*Letters in initials.*

*Sacred circles.*

*Cosmic weather.*

*Invisible liars.*

*Spirit guides.*

Why?

Because myth is easier than banality.

If the love was archetypal, then the loss was destiny.

If it was destiny, then I was not simply a woman who ran.

If it was cosmic, then it was not avoidant attachment and fear of permanence.

If it was sacred, then I did not have to look at my part.

Myth became anaesthetic.

It numbed the humiliation of rupture.

It protected me from the small, unromantic truth:

I did not know how to live in real life.

Real life is not a ring of trees.

It is rent.

Jealousy.

Conflict.

Repair.

Staying after the temperature drops.

I could ignite.

I could worship.

I could eroticise danger.

I could stand in storm.

I could not inhabit Tuesday.

So, when the relationship fractured, I wrapped it in gold.

I turned it into twin flame.

I turned him into archetype.

I turned myself into tragic heroine instead of frightened woman.

This is not self-condemnation. It is clarity.

Myth gave meaning to pain. But it also prevented integration. Because as long as it was legendary, I did not have to admit it was human.

And human love demands something harder than myth.

It demands embodiment without theatre. It demands staying present when there is no rainbow.

That is what I could not yet do. That is what this book is really about.

Not twin flames. Not prophecy. Not Cathy and Heathcliff.

But the long, slow work of thawing enough to live without needing the sky to split open.

# Chapter Fifteen: What Remains.

*Moonflower for the Love That Only Lived at Night*

*It opened in the dark, whispered its devotion, and vanished before the sun could see it.*

In those woods, a part of us became eternal.

Deeper parts of us, ghosts of who we once were lingered there; raising our golden child, making love on summer mornings, offering our praises to the gods.

We became part of the forest, woven into its pages like dried flowers pressed into the book of life.

When the gods led us to the life we were supposed to live, they filled my body with a light so powerful it was impossible to contain. It was golden, endless, and all-encompassing, and in that light, I became one with something greater.

Your ghost was there, Robert. I realised it had always been there, waiting in the glen.

The ghost of our younger selves still lived in the folds of the light, in the patterns of the wood.

We walked hand in hand within it, and nothing was lost.

The gods had always held us in their hands, even when we thought we'd been abandoned and had abandoned each other.

The darker details of the story unfold. The snowflake, the bark, the red berries, the shafts of sunlight. The gods leave their fingerprints on everything. The patterns of life itself, intricate and eternal, shimmer across all that we are. Even though love might seem lost, it is never gone; it becomes part of the pattern.

Like a flower pressed between the pages of a book, it is preserved; stored within the tapestry of life, it waits, unextinguished, eternal.

*Robert Joseph* - it remains.

Even when the loudness of the world drowns it out, even when the pettiness of human drama obscures it.

It exists in every moment shared, every touch, every creation that springs from it.

The gods themselves wove us into their story, into the chemistry of twin flames united and then torn apart. The clean fruit is transformed. Into the great, shimmering tapestry of existence; woven into the snowflakes, the bark, the pine needles, the light.

Though we may not hold it, we carry it always, pressed into the book of our lives, part of the gods' eternal pattern. Love is never lost.

*Dear RJ - it remains.*

**Author's Clinical Notes:**

In those woods, something did become eternal.

Not in the way I once believed; not in snowflakes and gods weaving us into constellations; but in the simpler, harsher way that memory fuses itself to the body.

We made a child there.

We lay beneath hail and sunlight and believed the sky had opened for us.

For years I told the story as if the forest had claimed us, as if we had become myth, preserved like pressed flowers in the great book of existence.

It was easier that way.

Easier than saying: he left.

Easier than saying: I ran.

Easier than admitting that love can be real and still not survive.

Charlie exists.

Not as symbol.

Not as prophecy.

Not as proof of twin flames.

He exists because two young, dysregulated people loved each other fiercely and did not know how to stay.

That is not divine tragedy.

It is human.

The woods remain.

The ring of trees remains.

The younger versions of us remain; suspended in that afternoon like light caught in resin.

But we are not there.

We grew older.

We broke.

We survived.

He never met his son.

That truth sits in me like a stone I cannot swallow.

But it is a human stone.

Not a cursed one.

Not a cosmic one.

Just grief.

Love is not never lost.

It changes form.

It becomes a child.

It becomes memory.

It becomes a scar that no longer bleeds.

And sometimes what remains is not destiny.

It is responsibility.

***

I can see now what I was doing.

I could not tolerate being rejected.

Not by him.

Not after everything.

So, I turned rejection into transcendence.

If he was my twin flame, then separation was spiritual.

If he moved on, then it was karmic timing.

If I saw him online smiling beside another woman, then that image had to be an illusion.

The alternative was unbearable:

He continued.

Without me.

He functioned.

Without myth.

Without eternal woods.

Without golden light.

And I; who had built cathedrals around the story; was left holding pressed flowers.

The pain of seeing him alive and not missing me was not cosmic.

It was primitive.

It was attachment injury.

It felt like having my mouth forced against a curb and my head struck from behind.

Not poetic.

Violent.

Humiliating.

Myth protected me from humiliation.

If the love was archetypal, then its ending was grand.

But if it was human, then I had to face something far smaller and far more brutal:

He chose differently.

He adapted.

He moved forward.

And I froze.

I do not say this with cruelty toward myself.

I say it with clarity.

For years I swung between two poles:

Romantic absolutism

and annihilating shame.

I did not know how to live in the middle.

I mythologised because myth makes pain feel meaningful.

But meaning is not the same as integration.

Integration is quieter.

It is accepting that:

We loved.

We broke.

We failed to repair.

He left.

I left.

A child was born.

Life continued.

No gods required.

What remains is not twin flame.

What remains is embodiment.

I no longer need the woods to shimmer to know that what happened mattered.

It mattered because it shaped me.

Not because it was eternal.

That distinction is everything.

Join Author Online.

Enjoyed this memoir? Be sure to leave a review! You can also preorder. And don't forget to download.

# About the Author

Christine Joanna Hart is a certified trauma psychotherapist specialising in adoption trauma, attachment wounds, destructive relationship patterns, shame, and parts-based therapy. Her work focuses on identity fragmentation, repetition compulsion, trauma bonding, and the unconscious forces that shape intimate relationships.

A Sunday Times bestselling author published by Hodder & Stoughton, Hart previously worked as an investigative journalist for the Daily Mail and Sunday Times, and has appeared on GMTV, BBC World Service, and Amazon Prime. Her Psychology of Trauma series explores how unresolved trauma drives power dynamics, attraction to narcissistic personalities, and the search for redemption through love.

She works with individuals, couples, and adolescents seeking deep psychological transformation.

For therapy enquiries and further writing, visit her website or Facebook page. :

Read more at www.christinejoannahart.com.

www.ingramcontent.com/pod-product-compliance
Lightning Source LLC
LaVergne TN
LVHW100314210926
848480LV00003B/1122